%/9 0/BC
PR
$33.00
3-5625

VIRGINIA COLONIAL ABSTRACTS

Vol. XXII
Lancaster County
1652 - 1655

Abstracted by
Beverley Fleet

D0700496

Baltimore
Genealogical Publishing Co.
1961

PREFACE

Old Mr. Vedder of New York contributed the following in regard to the importance of keeping one's mouth shut:
> "He comes from nearby Prattleville,
> Polonius is his name.
> Explaining the self evident,
> Is Polly's little game" - and so on.

With no desire to push Polly from his place, already greatly endangered by many a preface writer, nevertheless:

Lancaster County Court Order Book is one of our earliest items with many American foundations. Poppycock ! - any dunce should have brains enough to know that without any remarks on my part. Let's try again. The original is at Lancaster Court House. Just where it should be. It was an unpardonable old parcel of paper rags. Just what was to be expected. It has been restored by devoted and very generous Virginians. Again the self evident. There is a photostadt copy in the Archives Division of the Virginia State Library. This was obtained by my beloved (even if slightly sharp) old friend, the late Morgan Poitiaux Robinson. Of course he obtained the essential records first.

The original has 336 pages. These abstracts are of pages 1-243. Every name and date that I could read is included. I don't think there were as many as a dozen that were illegible. Perhaps I may be excused for not reading those torn away. To my surprise there was very little of that. Practically none. This book is said to be the most difficult item in the Virginia records. It is not. It is merely a question of adjusting your mind to the handwritings. This takes a little time I admit. Hurried students had simply best skip this mass of minor detail.

Now for what was not self evident. Just refer to the short memorandum for genealogists at the end of this volume.

                                                Beverley Fleet.

15 Sept 1944.

INDEX

Lancaster County Records

This list was prepared by the late Morgan Poitiaux Robinson for the
Archives Division of the Virginia State Library.

Deed Books

1	1652-1657	Deeds, etc. 336 p. no index. See General Index volume, p. 1-3
2	1654-1660	Deeds, etc. 393 p. Index both ways. See also General Index volume, p. 4-12
-	1660-1666	Where is it ? Probably some deeds are in Deeds, etc. p.399-458 which documents were re-recorded in accordance with the order appearing on p. 461. Also, there are probably some few deeds in Orders, etc. 1655-1666.
3	1666-1682	Deeds, etc. 452 p. Index seperate, but bound in photostat copy. See also General Index volume p. 12-15
4	1682-1687	Deeds,etc. 135 f. Index. See also General Index volume p. 16-17
5	1687-1700	Deeds, etc. 184 f. Index. See also General Index volume p. 19-21
-	1700-1701/2	Where is 22 Nov. 1700 - 10 March 1701/2 ? (Note that Wills etc. 1690-1709, f. 108, shows the record date "Mar. 11, 1701/2", but am unable to find any deeds immediately preceding this entry).
6	1701/2-1715	Deeds. 537 p. Index. See also General Index volume p. 21-24. (Note that the last record date (p. 537) is "2d July 1711", while later dates precede this entry).
7	1715-1728	Deeds. 360 p. Index. See also General Index volume p. 24-27
8	1727-1736	Deeds and Wills. 364 p. Index. See also General Index volume p. 27-28.
9	1736-1743	Deeds, etc. 344 p. Index. See also General Index volume p. 28-29. (Note that this volume and 14, below, show the following irregularities, - 9 Sept Court, 1743, is in vol.13, p.342-3 14 Oct Court, 1743, is in vol.14, f.1-2 11 Nov Court, 1743, is in vol.14. f.2-3 and vol.13. p.344)
10	1743-1750	Deeds and Wills. 325 f. Index. See also General Index volume, p. 29-31
11	1750-1758	Wills, etc. 324 f. Index. See also General Index volume, p. 31-33
12	1758-1763	Deeds and Wills. 257 f. Index. See also General Index volume, p. 33-34
13	1763-1764	Deeds and Wills. f.1-35. Index. See also General Index volume, p.35

Lancaster County Records
continued

Deed Books
14   1764-1770   Records (Deeds, etc.) 173 f. Index. See also
                   General Index volume p 35-37.
15   1770-1782   Deeds. 276 f. Index. See also General Index volume
                   p. 37-40.
16   1782-1793   Deeds, etc. 282 f. Index. See also General Index
                   volume p. 40-45.
-     1793-1803   Deeds, etc. 533 p. Index. See also General Index
                   volume p. 45-49. No photostat copy made for Archives
                   Div., Va. State Library. Original returned to Clerk's
                   Office, Lancaster Court House.
17   1652-1803   General Index volume. 150 p. "REVERSED. A General
                   Index to the Records of Lancaster county Court in
                   the State of Virginia completed this the 15th day
                   of September, 1806, p James Towles cl", - but
                   obviously not wholly contemporaneous.

Order Books

1   1652-1657   See Deeds No. 1
18   1656-1666   Orders. 388 p. (pages 378-384 blank). Skeleton
                   index.
19   1666-1680   Orders, etc. 541 p. No index.
20   1680-1686   Orders. 272 p. No index.
21   1686-1696   Orders. 183 f. No index.
22   1696-1702   Orders. 177 f. Index seperate, but bound in photo-
                   stat copy.
23   1702-1713   Orders. 478 p. No index.
24   1713-1721   Orders. 359 p. Index. Note - There is no letter
                   'G', although the serial numbers are unbroken,
                   while the absence of 'J' is accounted for by the
                   fact that this volume was not received by the
                   library; and, upon inquiry, the clerk says, under
                   date of Dec 27 1929 - "It may be that the books
                   you say are missing are combined with some volumes
                   of an earlier date". This notation means that the
                   original identification of these volumes was by
                   letter, rather than by number. The numbers shown
                   in this list were probably first used by the Va.
                   State Library.
25   1721-1729   Orders. 388 p. Index. For Orders of 1st May 1722
                   see pp. 337-8
26   1729-1743   Orders. 295 p. No index.
27   1752-1756   Orders. 454 p. Index.
28   1756-1764   Orders. 544 p. Index.

Lancaster County Records
continued

Order Books.

13	1764-1767	Records. (incl.orders) p. 1-268 (latter half) Index.
14	1767-1768	Records. (incl.orders) 86 p. (latter half). Index.
29	1768-1770	Orders. 88 f. Index. Unable to find Orders for June Court, 1770.
30	1770-1778	Orders. 451 p. Index.
31	1778-1783	Orders. f. 11-129. Index.
32	1783-1785	Orders. 131 f. Index.
33	1786-1789	Orders. 215 f. Index. The last dated entry on f. 215 is December 1788; but the clerk's signed memorandum at the bottom of the page says "Orders from the 12th of January, 1786, to Wednesday the 17th day of March, 1789". However, Jan-Mar 1789 is on f. 203-213, followed by the prior dates of Nov. and Dec. 1788 on f. 213-215, while there are other evidences of v. d.
-	1789-1792	Orders. 361 p. Indices (2) seperate. No photostat copies made of this or the two following volumes, because of lack of funds. Originals were returned to the clerk's office.
-	1792-1799	Orders. 530 p. Index. (See above)
-	1799-1801	Orders. 366 p. Index. " "

Will Books.

1	1652-1657	See Deeds No. 1
2	1654-1660	See Deeds No. 2
-	1660-1666	Where is it ? Probably some wills in Deeds No.2, 1654-1702, p 399-458, q. v., which documents were re-recorded in accordance with the order appearing on p. 461. Also, there are probably some few wills in Orders, etc., No. 18, 1656-1666.
3	1666-1682	See Deeds, etc. No.3
34	1674-1689	Wills, etc. 135 p. No index. See General Index volume p. 15-16.
35	1690-1709	Wills, etc. 139 f. No index. See General Index volume p. 17-19.
36	1709-1727	Wills, etc. 560 p. Index seperate but bound in photostat copy.
8	1727-1736	See Deeds and Wills No.8

Lancaster County Records
continued

Will Books.

9	1736-1743	See Deeds No. 9. Note: This volume and No. 14 below, show the following irregularities: 9 Sept. 1743 Court is in Vol.13 p. 342-3 14 Oct. 1743 Court is in Vol.14 f. 1-2 11 Nov. 1743 Court is in Vol.14 f. 2-3 and in Vol. 13 p. 344.
10	1743-1750	See Deeds and Wills No. 10
11	1750-1758	Wills. 324 f. Index. See also General Index volume p. 31-33
12	1758-1763	See Deeds and Wills No. 12
13	1763-1764	See Deeds and Wills No. 13
14	1764-1770	Records. See listed under Deed Books, No.14
37	1770-1783	Wills, etc. 271 f. Index.
38	1783-1795	Wills, etc. 312 p. Index.

In the above list I've omitted certain of Mr. Robinson's technicalities in that they confuse me and I think would confuse others. The system in the Virginia State Library has been changed or rather modernized. It is easier to ask for these volumes by date rather than by number. Or do as I do. The Lancaster records are on the open shelves in the reading room of the Archives Division, and plainly marked. Point your finger at the one you want and say "Please give me that". The quick and polite assistants immediately put it upon a rack on your table.

By the way, these racks, the best I ever had to work with, were made at the Virginia State Penitentiary right over the hill.

B.F.

Lancaster County
Court Orders
1652 - 1655

Abby, Willm. To pay levy for 1 titheable to Wm Neesham. 7 Dec 1655.
    p. 237
Aberdine, Ja:, Headright of Epe Boney. 10 Jan 1652/3. p.26
Ackeen, Jno. Headright of Tobie Horton. 6 Aug 1655. p.208
Adams, Geo. Headright of Geo Taylor. 6 Oct 1654. p.162
Adawell family detail. See entry Saml Gooch. 16 Mar 1652/3. p.123
Adrye, Elinor, Headright of Toby Smith. 6 Oct 1652. p.16
Aduston, Jno. Wit Hackery to Burroughs. Exact date not shown. Betw 1st
    Sept 1651 and 16 June 1653. p.148
Akin see Ackeen
Aklison, Jas. (or Allison) Given a calf by Abra Moone. 18 Oct 1653.
    p. 103
    Headright of Abra Moone. 7 Aug 1654. p.153
Allanson, Tho. Wit deed Clapham to Fleet. 30 June 1655. p.229
Allen, Andrew. Headright of Rice Jones. 6 Aug 1652. p.2
Allen, Charles. "Receaved by me Charles Allen and Mary my wife daughter
    of Nicho Dale late deceased of Rich Paratt and Sara his wife the
    relict and Administratrix of my said father Nick Dale" certain
    cattle "given by my fathers will and afterwards given me by the
    (said) Rich Parratt and Sarah my father and mother in law".
    Wit: Fra Holland, Robert Parr. Dated 23 Oct 1649. Recorded 10th
    Apl 1653. p.48
Allen, Marga: Headright of Jno Weir. 6 Oct 1654. p.162
Allison see Aklison.
Allison, Tho. Headright of Capt Hen. Fleet. 6 June 1655. p.198
Anderton, Jno. Wit. Brocas to Chicheley. 17 Nov 1652. p.190
Armall, Anthoine. Wit deed Meriwether to Hagett. 3 Oct 1654. p.178
Armeraud, Rev. Jno. This name also appears as Jno Almoner and as
    Armourier prior to 1651 in Northampton Co. The entry here is "The
    Court hath ordered that all those that are indebted to Mr
    Armeraud late Minister of Wickocomicoe by subscriptions under
    their hands shall pay and satisfy the same to Coll Wm Clayborne
    Esqr or his assignes". 9 Dec 1653. p.100
Armstrong, Robt. To pay levy on 3 tytheables to Mr And: Gilson. 6th
    Feb 1654/5. p.174
Arundell, Mary. See entry Jno Paine. 6 Aug 1652. p.3
    Summoned with Tho Brooks for "Incontineurie", which we may presume
    means incendiary or arson. 6 Oct 1652. p.17
Aschley, Xper: with Tho Best buys 350 acres from Edw James. 28 August
    1654. The record actually shows this as dated 1651. pp 184-5
Ashley, Christopher (shown here as Exper Asshley). See entry Tho
    Roots. 6 Feb 1653/4. p.139
Astley, Jno. To pay levy on 1 tytheable to Mr Tho Bearn (Bourne) 24th
    Oct 1653. p.92
Ashley, John. Grant dated 10 Mar 1653/4 to John Ashley and Thomas
    Hamper, 300 acres on N. side Peacketanke River. They sell this
    land to Vincent Stanford 10 Sept 1654. Wit: Hen Fleet. Jesper x
    Griffin. p.188

Ashley, Roger. Wit deed Reade to Kempe. 16 May 1654. p.159
Astell, Jas. P of A dated 14 Jan 1650/1 from Wm Harris. See entry Hen
    Monford. 12 Aug 1650. p.83
Atkins see Attoins.
Attoins, Francis. Headright of Mr Tho Hawkins. 6 Aug 1655. p 208
Atkinson possibly Aklison.
Attawaye, Wm. Headright of Abra Moone. 7 Aug 1654. p 153
Attawell, Fra. Daughter in law of Edw Grime. Bequest from him. 1 Aug
    1653. p 124
Attawell family detail. See entry Saml Gooch. 16 Mar 1652/3. p 123
    Also see entry Tho Roots chirurgeon. 14 Oct 1653. p 121
Attawell see Hadwell.
Avwen, Jno. (?). Headright of Danl Welch. 6 Aug 1653. p 62
Axome, Richd. With Tho Godwin patents 1000 acres in Rappa river. 22nd
    May 1650. p 168
Ayres, Jno. To pay levy on 3 tytheables to Mr Geo Taylor. 6 Feb 1654/5.
    p. 174
Ayres see Eyres.

Bacon, Tho. Inquiry of the manner of living of his wife with Hum
    Hagett, she being hired to him, to be made by Mr Edmond Kempe.
    6 June 1655. p 196
    Ordered to do work due Hum: Hagett, his person to be secured
    while the work is being done. Hagett to put up bond to keep the
    peace. 6 June 1655. p 196
    Difference with Humphrey Hagett settled. Hagett putting away
    Bacon's wife and delivering her goods to her. 6 June 1655. p 197
    Signing with mark he wit deed Humph Haggett to Charles Hill. 12th
    April 1655. p 207
Bagnall, Mr James.
    Justice. 1 July 1652. p.1
    "Commissioner of the Quorum" to swear Mr Antho Jackman as Constable
    for S. side Rappa River. 6 Aug 1652. p 3
    Justice. 10 Jan 1652/3. p 23
    Pd 100 lb tobo from County levy for a wolf. 10 Jan 1652/3. p 29
    Justice. 6 Apl 1653. p 43
    Justice. 6 Aug 1653. p 61
    See entry 'Muster'. 8 Aug 1653. p 65
    Justice. 24 Oct 1653. p 89
    To collect annual levy from these families for 35 tytheables. Mr
    Jones 4. Anth: Jackman 2. Mr Rich: Loes 3. Robt Bryan 2. Wm Bent
    2. Hen Dedman 3. Tho Griffin and Mynor 2. Mr Bagnall himselfe 5.
    Mr. Paine 5. Jno Bebey 2. Wm Jno'son 2. Mr Coxes family 2. Thomas
    Vaughan 1. 24 Oct 1653. p 94
    To be pd 300 lb tobo from Co. levy for 2 wolves heads. 24th Oct
    1653. p 95
    Justice. 7 Aug 1654. p 151

Bagnall, Mr James,
    To appraise the est of Tho Steephens dec'd. 7 Aug 1654. p 153
    Justice. 6 Oct 1654. p 162
    Justice. 6 Feb 1654/5. p 171
    His name, with Mr Toby Smith and Mr David Fox,presented for
    election of sheriff. 6 Feb 1654/5. p 172
    To collect levy for 33 tytheables including 4 of his own. 6 Feb.
    1654/5. p 174
    Justice. 6 June 1655. p 196
    Reference to his plantation. See entry 'Markets'. 6 June 1655.
    p. 201
    Buys 200 acres from Abra Moone. See entry his name. 22 May 1655.
    p. 207
    Justice. 6 Aug 1655. p 207
    Certificate for land for importing 12 persons. 6 Aug 1655. p 208
    To receive levy for 27 tytheables from 11 persons incl 6 tytheables
    of his own. 7 Dec 1655. p 236
    Wit: Edgecombe's public apology to Fantleroy. 15 Sept 1655. p 243
    Justice. 6 Jan 1655/6. p 244
Bagwell, Mr. To pay annual levy to Mr Rd Perrot on 4 tytheables. 24th
    Oct 1653. p 93
Baker, Hen. Headright of V Stanford. 6 June 1655. p 198
Baldwin, John
    In County levy pmt to be made "to John Bauldwin for the burgesses
    charges and to be discompted on their bill" 918 lb tobo. 24th Oct
    1653. p 90
    To be pd 1092 lb tobo from County levy by Mr Da Fox "for the
    burgesses Charge and to be discharged upon their bill". 24th Oct
    1653. p 91
    In the annual levy Mr Geo Taylor is instructed "to pay Jno
    Baldwin for the burgesses charge and to be discharged upon his
    bill 820 lb tobo", etc. 24 Oct 1653. p 92
    To be pd 2164 lb tobo collected from annual levy by Mr Jno Cox.
    24 Oct 1653. p 93
    To be pd 349 lb tobo from County levy by Capt Hen Fleet. The Fleet
    entry reads "To himself for caske upon the Burgesses bill to Jo:
    Baldwyn". 7 Dec 1655. p 235
Ball, Tho of Northampton Co., Virginia, mariner, buys 350 acres on N.
    side of E branch of Corotomen River from Dr Jno Edwards. 31 Dec
    1653. p 149
Ball, Wm. Wit deed Fleet to Sharpe. 10 Dec 1653. p 132. Also wit deed
    Fleet to Sharpe, no date shown but betw 1 Aug 1652 and 11 Dec
    1654. p 186
Baning, Ebber (prob Ebe Bonnison) Buys 350 acres known as Muskeeto
    Poynt from Ever Petterson. 29 Oct 1652. p 39
Banister possibly appears here as Bemister.
Barber, Edm. Headright of Capt More Fantleroy. 10 Jan 1652/3. p 27
Barnes, Jno. Headright of Abra Weeks. 6 Oct 1653. p 77
Barres, Hugh. Headright of Wm Brocas. 6 Oct 1652. p 16

Bartian, Mary. Headright of Sir H Chisley (Chicheley).10 Jan 1652/3.
    p 27
Bartlet, Alex. Headright of Tho Griffin. 10 Jan 1652/3. p 24
Bartlett, Walter. Headright of Jas Bonner. 25 Oct 1655. p 210
Bartlett see Bertlet
Batersby, Michaell of Lancaster Co, Rappahannock, cooper. Gives a red
    heifer to Wm Newsan and Jno Pinn jointly. Wit: Howell Powell. Jno
    Walker. 21 Mar 1652/3. p 66
Batesby, Miles. See Wm Newsam et als. 29 Jan 1649/50. p 69
Batte, Wm. Wit Petterson to Baning. 29 Oct 1652. p 39
Battle, Mary. Headright of Capt Hen Fleet. 6 June 1655. p 198
Bayley, Joan. Headright of Wm Thomas. 10 Jan 1652/3. p 24
Baytson, Nathl. At 3 suits of Capt More Fantilroy returned "non est
    inventus". 6 Aug 1652. p 3
        Several actions agt him at suit of Capt More Fantilroy. Now order-
        ed to pay 5515 lb tobo and costs of suits. 10 Jan 1652/3. p 26
        Judgment agt him to Capt More Fantilroy for 96 arms length of
        Roanoke, 5515 lb tobo, a gun sold by him to the Indians, etc. 10th
        Jan 1652/3. p 28
Beach, George
        Wit. Powell to Sneade. 14 Mar 1652/3. p 52
        Wit Howell Powell to Charles Snead. 5 Mar 1652/3. pp 54-55
        To pay levy on 2 tytheables to Mr Tho Brice. 24 Oct 1653. p 91
        Summoned to answer misdemeanors toward Ha- Harison and her brother.
        6 June 1654. p 146
        To pay levy for 3 tytheables to Mr Tho Brice. 6 Feb 1654/5. p 174
        His servant, Robt Knopp, ordered to serve him 6 months extra for
        absenting himself. 7 Dec 1655. p 231
        To pay levy for 3 titheables to Wm Neesham. 7 Dec 1655. p 237
Bealle, Benj: Wit receipt Woodward to Williamson. 4 Dec 1653. p 87
Beare, Tho. Headright of Capt Hen: Fleet. 24 Oct 1653. p 89
Bebey, John. To pay annual levy to Mr Jas Bagnall for 2 tytheables. 24
    Oct 1653. p 94
        To be paid from County levy "for one wolves head 0150 lb tobo" 24
        Oct 1653. p 95
        To pay levy on 1 tytheable to Mr Ja Bagnall. 6 Feb 1654/5. p 174
        To appraise estate of Paul Brewer. 6 June 1655. p 201
        (here as Jo Bibby) To pay levy on 1 tytheable to Mr Smith. 7 Dec
        1655. p 239
Beete, Hen. Headright of Capt Hen Fleet. 24 Oct 1653. p 89
Bell, John. Order that his corn, clothes, etc., be pd by Mr Rice Jones,
    he having finished his time. 10 Jan 1652/3. p 24
        To pay levy on 1 tytheable to Mr Tho Bourne. 6 Feb 1654/5. p 174
        To pay levy on 2 tytheables to Mr Bagnall. 7 Dec 1655. p 236
        To pay levy on 1 tytheable to Mr Kempe. 7 Dec 1655. p 239
Bemister, Tho. See entry Abra Weeks. 6 Feb 1653/4. p 137
Bence, Wm. Wit Bennett to Loes. 4 June 1652. p 46
Bendridge, Philip. Wit deed of gift Moone to Allison. 18 Oct 1653.
    p 103
Bendry, Adrian. Signs schedule of Capt Wm Brocas' estate. Recorded 7th
    May 1655. p 191

Bendye, Andrew. Headright of Sir H Chisley (Chicheley) 10 Jan 1652/3.
    p 27
Bennett, Edw. Headright of Edwin Conway. 6 Aug 1653. p 62
Benet, Ja: see 'Muster'. 8 Aug 1653. p 65
Bennett, Richard. Now I am not sure but it appears to me as though
    there were more than one person of this name in these records.
    The Governor and perhaps two others. Therefore each entry will
    be shown as clearly as I can. As one of the numerous descendants
    of the Puritan Governor I am aware that no satisfactory life of
    this person has ever been published. B.F.
Bennett, Richd, merchant. Bond 8337 lb tobo from Henry Dedman. 4 June
    1652. p 4
Bennett, Richd. merchant. Bond 12000 lb tobo from Rice Jones of Rappa:
    7 June 1652. p 6
Bennett, Richard of Virginia. merchant. Sells Rice Jones of Rappa: abt
    600 or 700 acres, part of a patent dated 4 of Nov 1642. Wit: W
    Clayborne, Tho Brice. 7 June 1652. p 8
Bennett, Richd:, merchant. Bond 40000 lb tobo to protect him as surety
    for Epa Lawson in debt to Symon Cuerzee. 13 Apl 1651. p 9
Bennett, Ri. Wit deed Burbage to Fox. 5 June 1652. p 14
Bennett, Richd. Sells 550 acres, part of patent of 4 Nov 1642 to Hen
    Dedman. 4 June 1652. p 21
Bennett, Richd. Sells 250 acres on S side Rappahannock River to Antho
    Jackman. 4 June 1652. p 22
Behnett, Rd of Virginia, merchant. Assignment to Wm Clapham the
    younger, all right in a mortgage dated 13 April 1651 given by
    Mr Epa Lawson deceased, for 40000 lb tobo on 2000 acres in Rappa:
    to be disposed of thus: 1000 acres to Richard Lawson, the other
    1000 acres to Elizabeth daughter of said Epa Lawson in trust till
    she be 15 years of age. Witness, Richard Lawson. 12th Sept 1652.
    p 31
    Further, another patent of 1000 acres lying below, not included
    in the mortgage, to be for 'the child' in lieu of the 1000 acres
    belonging to Wm Clapham. Wit: John Scapes. 5 Oct 1652. p 31
Bennett, Ri. A letter from him to Mr Toby Smith regarding Wm Clapham
    and the Lawson estate. 12 Sept 1652. p 32
Bennett, Mr Rich: named as Admr in will of Epa: Lawson. 31 Mar 1652.
    p 34
Bennett, Ri, Governor, etc. Orders that Clement Thrush have admr of
    the estate of Ro Vivian deceased. 10 Dec 1652. p 35
Bennett, Richd of Virginia, merchant. Sells Richard Loes 300 acres,
    part of a patent of 2000 acres dated 4 Nov 1642. This land in
    Rappahannock on S side and adj land of Anthony Jackman to the
    East and the land of the widow Marsh to the West. Wit: Wm Bence,
    W Claiborne. 4 June 1652. p 46
Bennett, Richard. "The County of Lancaster Dr to the Ho'ble Rich
    Bennett Esqr Governor 13260 pounds tobacco". 6 Feb 1654/5. p 174
Bennett, Ri. Signs patent to Tho Lucas. 7 June 1652. p 221
Bennett, Mr Richd Esqr. Formerly sold 700 acres to Ephr: Lawson. 30th
    June 1655. p 229

Bent, Wm. (or Bout ?) To pay annual levy to Mr Jas Bagnall on 2
    tytheables. 24 Oct. 1653. p 94
Berkeley, Sir William
    Signs patent (shown here as 'William Barckeley') to Tho Lucas.
    7 Aug 165- (blotted but prior to 1654). p 220
    Signs patent to Jno Bond. 29 Feb 1650/1. p 240
Berrey, Hen: Headright of Mr Row Lawson. 6 Feb 1654/5. p 172
Bertlet, Ann. Headright of Fra Gower. 8 Dec 1653. p 96
Best, Jno. See entry Tho Roots. 6 Feb 1653/4. p 139
Best, Tho. With Xp'er Aschley buys 350 acres from Edw James. The date
    is prob 28 Aug 1654 but the record actually shows it as of 1651.
    pp 184-5
Best, Tho. Buys 350 acres from Edw James 5 Sept 1654/5. Sells it to
    Tho Wms and Alexr Porteus 6 Feb 1654/5. p 184
Billingsby, Major Jno. Appraises estate of Epaph: Lawson dec'd. 2 June
    1652. p 10
Bishop, Cyprian. To pay levy on 2 tytheables to Mr Ja Bagnell. 6 Feb
    1654/5. p 174
    To pay levy on 1 tytheable to Mr Bagnall. 7 Dec 1655. p 236
Blacke, Jno. Headright of Sir Hen Chisley (Chicheley) 10 Jan 1652/3
    p 27
Blake, Elyas. Ordered to pay Ra Paine 100 lb tobo for loss of time in
    suit betw Blake and Jno Phillips. 9 Dec 1653. p 100
    To pay levy on 3 tytheables to Capt Hen: Fleet. 6 Feb 1654/5.
    p 174
Blake, Jno. Signs schedule of Capt Wm Brocas' estate. Recorded 7 May
    1655. p 191
Bland, Fra: Headright of Capt Hen: Fleet. 24 Oct 1653. p 89
Bland, Perigrine. His land was on - side of Peacketanke River, across
    the creek from 600 acres granted George Reade and on 16 May 1654
    assigned to Edmond Kemp. 22 Oct 1651. p 159
Boeman, Tho. (or Booman ?). Dif betw him and Jno Cox to next Court.
    7 Dec 1655. p 232
Boimer, Ja: To pay annual levy to Mr Jno Cox on 2 tytheables. 24 Oct
    1653. p 93
Bonas, John. Headright of Epe Boney. 10 Jan 1652/3. p 26
Bond, Major John. Of Isle of Wight Co. Patent to him 760 acres on N.
    side of Rappahannook River in Corretomen River on Eastermost
    branch on S side thereof. Adj land of Geo Taylor, the river, etc.
    For transportation of 15 persons into this colony. 29 Feb 1650/1.
    p 240
    He assigns above to Jno Meredith, excepting 160 acres which
    belongs to Eliz Hutchins the wife of Wm Hutchins. Dated 4 Dec
    1655. Recorded 5 Jan 1655/6. p 241
    Whereas a dif betw Major Jno Bond of Isle of Wight Co and John
    Meredith concerning land on Corotomen River has been settled. Bond
    now with consent of Meredith, deeds to Eliz Greene als Hutchins
    160 acres, the upper part of the patent of 760 acres. Signed John
    Bond. Wit: Howell Powell, John Meredith, Jo: x Mungoe. Recorded
    5 Jan 1655/6. p 241

Bonner, Jas. Patent dated 15 Sept 1651, 300 acres on S side Rappa:
adj N.W. on land of Tho Godwin, S.E. agst land of Nicho: Dale.
Bonner assigns this land to Wm Tignor. Wit: Geo Waddinge, Rich
Lake. 6 June 1654. p 147
> To pay levy on 3 tytheables to Mr John Cox. 6 Feb 1654/5. p 174
> His land abt 6 miles up the Rappahannock River on the South side.
> 10 Feb 1653/4. p 178
> Claims 200 acres for importing James Bonner, Walter Bartlett, Jno
> Bradshaw and Wm Fisher. 25 Oct 1655. p 210
> To pay annual levy on 5 titheables to Wm Leech. 7 Dec 1655. p 236

Bonnison, Epe. A Dutchman. His name appears in various spellings. Thus:
Boner, Epe. Certificate for importing 6 persons: Silvester Liner (?),
Ja: Aberdine, Ever Peeterson, Dorick Jonson, John Bonas, Epe Boner.
10 Jan 1652/3. p 26

Bonison, Eby. Wit: Seamor to Carter. 16 March 1652/3. p 47

Bonnison, Epe: Entered here as "Epe the Dutchman". To pay annual levy
on 2 tytheables to Mr Row: Lawson. 24 Oct 1653. p 90

Bonney, Epe. Dif betw him and Elyas Edmonds to next Court. 9 Dec 1653.
p 99

Bonnison and Bonney evidently different spellings of the same name.
See entry Elias Edmonds. 6 Feb 1653/4. p 137

Bonison, Ebey. To pay annual levy on 4 tytheables to Capt Hen: Fleet.
6 Feb 1654/5. p 174

Booth, Mr. To pay levy on 7 tytheables to Wm Neesham. 7 Dec 1655.
p. 237

Booth, Humph: Wit: deed Paine to Snead. 21 Oct 1654. p 183

Booth, Wm. Assigned to Capt Hen: Fleet a debt of 1302 lb tobo due from
estate of Rd Lake. Prior to 6 Feb 1654/5. p 173

Borough, Thos. Sells Tho Hopkins 300 acres known as 'Narow Neck'. Wit:
Edw: Conway. Jno Edwards. 5 Feb 1654/5. p 180

Bourough, Tho. Buys 300 acres from David Fox 3 Mar 1653/4. Sells it to
Tho Hopkins. 5 Feb 1654/5. p 180

Boswell, Edw:
> Constable for this year. 6 Apl 1653. p 44
> Wit: Pedro and Davis to White and Welch. 23 May 1652. p 45
> Patents 150 acres on S side Sunderland Creek adj land of Denis
> Coniers and Evan Davies, land of Bartram Hobert, etc. 5 March
> 1651/2. Boswell assigns this to Jno Pedro and Evan Davies. Wit:
> by Tho: Griffin. Rich Cole. One neck of land sold to Rich White
> and John Welch is taken out of this patent of Pedro and Davies.
> 16 May 1653.   Evan Davies assigns all right in above to John
> Pedro. Wit: Rich Cole. Tho Griffeth (sic).   John Pedro assigns
> his right in above to Capt Wm Brocas Esqr excepting the neck
> already assigned to White and Welch. Wit: Cuth Potter. Abra:
> Moone. 13 Nov 1653. p 118

Boswell, Edw: Land on S side Rappahannock granted him 5 March 1651/2
sold to Jno Pedro and Evan Davies. 18 Nov 1653. p 133

Boswell, Edw: Complains agt Abra Moone, etc. 6 June 1654. p 145

Boswell, Edw: To be pd balance of 246 lb tobo, now in hands of Capt
    Fantleroy, of a debt of 3500, assigned from Major Jno Carter to
    Wm Neesam and Jno Merriman, as due from the estate of Epa Lawson.
    6 June 1654. p 146

Boswell, Mr. To pay levy on 4 tytheables to Mr Rd Perrott. 6 Feb 1654/5.
    p 174

Boswell's plantation. See entry Denis Coniers. 16 Oct 1652. p 49

Bourne, Thomas.
    This entry under name of Mr Tho Bearn. He to collect annual levy
    on 8 tytheables from 5 persons, viz. Himself 3, Mr Leake 2, Row
    Haddaway 1. Jno Astley 1, Rich Hacker 1. 24 Oct 1653. p 92
    Buys 500 acres on S side Mulford Haven from Abra Moone. See entry
    his name. 26 May 1652. p 106
    To be pd from County levy for 4 wolves heads. 6 Feb 1653/4. p 139
    To appraise estate of Rd Lake dec'd. 6 Oct 1654. p 162
    To collect levy on 21 tytheables incl 5 of his own family. 6 Feb
    1654/5. p 174
    The suit of Abra Moone agst him to next Court. 6 June 1655. p 197
    Trespassed against on South side of River by Wickocomikoe Indians.
    Capt Hen: Fleet to demand satisfaction for him. 6 June 1655. p 198
    Wit: P of A Whitty to Smith. 19 May 1654. p 222
    To pay levy on 6 tytheables to Mr Kompe. 7 Dec 1655. p 239

Bowler, Tho: Wit P of A Jno Jefrys of London to Col Rd. Lee. 7th Feb
    1652/3. p 112

Boyer, Andrew.
    Nonsuit to him and his wife agt Rd Flinte. 6 Apl 1653. p 43
    Action against him by the Commonwealth, he having shot and hurt
    an Indian against the law of the country. Ordered to pay a 'matche
    coate' to Mr David Fox for the Indian. 6 Apl 1653. p 43
    To pay levy on 2 tytheables to Mr Row Lawson. 24 Oct 1653. p 90
    Described in entry as 'planter'. Leases 350 acres on East side of
    Northwest branch of Corotomen River from Jno Nicholls. 22nd Dec
    1652. p 114
    To pay levy to V Stanford. 7 Dec 1655. p 235

Bradshaw, Mr. To pay levy on 6 tytheables to Mr Ja Williamson. 6th
    Feb 1654/5. p 174

Bradshaw, Edw. Judgmt agt him - lb tobo to Wm Cotton. This entry all
    but illegible and is subject to correction. 6 Aug 1655. p 208

Bradshaw, Jno. Headright of Jas Bonner. 25 Oct 1655. p 210

Brathard, Jno. Headright of Capt Hen Fleet. 24 Oct 1653. p 89

Brathat, Jno. Assigned land by Wm Roughton. 25 Oct 1655. p 215
    Buys 300 acres from Wm Raughton. 27 Sept 1655. p 216

Breamer, Mr (Tho). Dif betw him and Mr Cox to next Court. 7 Dec 1655.
    p 232
    Has David Phelps arrested, but not appearing against him is non-
    suited. 7 Dec 1655. p 232

Brecknock Bay. In Rappahannock River. Adj land of Tho Godwin and Jno
    Lanman. 22 May 1650. p 168

Bredwell, Bridget. Headright of Robt Tomlyn. 6 Oct 1653. p 78
Breian, Wm. Judgt agt him to Wm Cotton for - lb tobo. This entry almost
    illegible. Subject to correction. 6 Aug 1655. p 208
Brent, Hugh. Certificate for transportation of 5 persons. 'his owne',
    Jno Noble, Robt Warner, Jno Girton, Mary Othersone (?). 6 Febry
    1654/5. p 171.
    Buys 200 acres in Fleet's Bay from Jno Sharp. 11 Dec 1654. p 187
    This entry as 'Hough Brent'. Wit deed Clapham to Fleet. 30th June
    1655. p 229
Brent, Jno. Shown in entry as 'Brint'. Headright of Capt Hen: Fleet.
    24 Oct 1653. p 89
    To pay levy on 2 tytheables to Capt Hen: Fleet. 6 Feb 1654/5.
    p 174.
Brent fling and Dod. 3 tytheables on Co levy list. 24 Oct 1653. p 90
Brewer, Paul. Also appears as Paule Brewer.
    Judgt to him agst Abra Moone 600 lb tobo. 6 Apl 1654. p 140
    Admr of his estate to Wm Jno'son. 6 June 1655. p 196
    A debt agst his estate, 700 lb tobo, assigned by Wm Johnson to
    Mr Tho Griffin. 6 June 1655. p 197
    His funeral charges, 750 lb tobo, to be pd to Oliver Segar. 6th
    June 1655. p 197
    His estate to be adm'rd by Mr Jno Cox, or he failing in proof by
    Wm Jno'son. 6 June 1655. p 201
    His estate to be pd 232 lb tobo by Mr Jo Cox. 25 Oct 1655. p 211
    His admr, Wm Johnson, to be pd 575 lb tobo by Mr Jackman. 25th
    Oct 1655. p 211
Brewton, Jno. Headright of Abra Moone. 7 Aug 1654. p 153
Brice. This name also appears as Bries, Bryes, etc., etc.
Bries, Geo. The whole estate of Tho Meads now in his (Bries') hands to
    be delivered to Mr Wm Underwood, guardian of Meads. 7 Dec 1655.
    p 233
Bryes, Geo: To pay levy on 2 tytheables to Mr Wm Underwood. 7 Dec 1655.
    p 234
Brice, Mrs Martha. See entry Jno Paine. 6 Aug 1652. p 3
Brice, Mr Tho: Justice. 6 Aug 1652. p 2
    The Court held at his house. 6 Aug 1652. p 2
    As "Commissioner of the Quorum" to swear Wm Clapham Sr as Constable
    on North side of Rappa: River. 6 Aug 1652. p 3
    Wit: bond Rice Jones to Rd Bennett. 7 June 1652. p 6
    Wit: deed Rd Bennett to Rice Jones. 7 June 1652. p 8
    All suits betw him and Wm Thomas and Jane his wife to next Court.
    6 Oct 1652. p 15
    His suit agst Wm Thomas dismissed. 6 Oct 1652. p 15
    Order that Wm Thomas pay him a debt of 711 lb tobo. 10 Jan 1652/3.
    p 27
    Is pd 1000 lb tobo from County levy. 10 Jan 1652/3. p 29
    "It is ordered that on the first of May ther be a meeting of the
    Inhabitants at the house of Mr Tho: Brice to chuse vestrymen and
    Churchwardens". 6 Apl 1653. p 44

Brice, Mr. Tho: See entry 'Muster'. 8 Aug 1653. p 65

Brice, Thos of Lancaster Co., gent., sells John Paine of same Co., a
neck of land beginning at a creek called' hapie Harbor', down the
side of the main river, etc. A creek dividing this land from
Poplar Neck, owned by sd Tho Brice, etc. This deed wit by Tho.
Roots. John Phillips. 25 July 1653. p 67
Subp: to appear as witness for Tho Paine agst Wm Dedman and did
not appear. Fined 300 lb tobo for Contempt. 6 Oct 1653. p 78
Ordered to report on boundries betw Tho Paine and Hen: Dedman. 6th
Oct 1653. p 78
Justice. 24 Oct 1653. p 89
To collect levy on W side 'Cossatawomen' (Corotomen) to his own
family for 42 tytheables including 6 tytheables due from himself.
24 Oct 1653. p 91
Justice. 6 Feb 1653/4. p 137
Justice. 7 Mar 1653/4. p 142
To collect levy for 58 tytheables incl 9 tytheables of his own
family. 6 Feb 1654/5. p 174
Arrested in 2 actions by Jas Yeates for detaining his crop, etc.
Ordered to pay Yeates 50 lb tobo upon nonsuit. 25 Oct 1655. p 213
Justice. 7 Dec 1655. 231
Suit betw him and James Yates to next Court. 7 Dec 1655. p 232
Levies to be collected by him last year to be collected now by
Wm Neesom. 7 Dec 1655. p 232
To pay levy on 7 tytheables to Wm Neesham. 7 Dec 1655. p 237
Justice. 6 Jan 1655/6. p 244

Bridges, Richd of Lancaster Co buys with Tho Pattison, 200 acres from
Tho Keds. 16 Apl 1655. p 219

Brint, Jno. Headright of Capt Hen: Fleet. 24 Oct 1653. p 89

Britten, Edwd. Wit agreemt Littlepage with Cox. 16 Jan 1653/4. p 104

Broadherst, Ralph. Headright of Toby Smith. 6 Oct 1652. p 16

Broadrib, Joan. Headright of Clemt Thrush. 6 Oct 1652. p 15

Brocas, Mrs Elnor. Delivers a cow to her neice Eltonhead Conway. 7 May
1653. p 69

Brocas, Mrs Tabitha. Headright of Capt Wm Brocas. 6 Oct 1652. p 16

Brocas, William. 'Capt Wm Brocas Esqr". This combination of a military
title and Esqr indicates membership in the King's Council.
Buys land on Sunderland Creek from Jno Pedro. 13 Nov 1653. p 118
See entry Sir Hen: Chicheley. 18 Apl 1654. p 129

Brocas, Capt William. Grant of 190 acres on S side of Rappa:, N.NW on
land of Denis Coniers and Evan Davies and a swamp at the head of
Obart's Creek, S. E. on land of Mr Bartram Obert, etc. 150 acres
part of above was formerly granted to Edwd Boswell on 5 Mar 1651/2
and assigned by him to Evan Davies and Jno Pedro, which Davies
assigned to Pedro and Pedro to Brocas. 18 Nov 1653. p 133. Brocas
now assigns his right in the land to Sir Henry Chicheley knt, ex-
cept a neck of land sold to Rich: White and now seated by him.
Wit: Martha Conway. Hen: Waldron. 28 Jan 1653/4. Sir Hen Chicheley
re-assigns the foregoing patent. Wit: Cuth Potter. 6 Feb 1653/4.
p 133

Brocas, Capt Wm Esqr. To pay levy on 12 tytheables to Mr Jno Cox. 6th
  Feb 1654/5. p 174
Brocas, Capt Wm Esqr. Deceased. On 7 Nov 1652 he made over to Sir Hen:
  Chicheley, Knt., his whole estate for the use of Mrs Elnor Brocas
  his then wife. The Court orders administration to Mrs Elenor
  Brocas and that the estate be appraised by Mr Edmond Kemp, Mr Row:
  Burnham, Mr Richd Perrott, Wm Leech, Mr Fra: Coale and Mr Barthr
  Horbartt. 7 May 1655. p 189
Brocas, Capt Wm. Makes over his estate to Sir Hen: Chicheley for the
  use of Mrs Elenor Brocas. Wit Edwin Conoway. John Anderton. 17th
  Nov 1652. p 190
Brocas, Capt Wm. A schedule of his estate. A number of handsome items
  listed. Signed by Jno Blake, Andrian Bendry, George Hickson. Sub-
  mitted with deed of trust dated 17 Nov 1652. Certified by Toby
  Smith. Recorded 7 May 1655. p 191
Brocas, Capt Wm. A servant in his estate, Geo Hickson (see foregoing
  entry) to serve 2 1/2 years. 6 June 1655. p 202
Brocas, Capt Wm. Deceased. Inventory of his estate (most interesting).
  Signed Edm Kempe, Row Burnham, Fra: Coale, Bartram Hobart, Wm
  Leech. 14 May 1655. p 202
Brocas, Capt Wm Esqr. A plantation, formerly his, mortgaged by Thomas
  Carter to John Carter. 18 Sept 1655. p 228
Brocas, Capt Wm. Certificate for importing 16 persons including 6
  negroes. 6 Oct 1652. p 16
Brocas, Capt. His house. See entry Denis Coniers. "26 March 1653".p 50
Brocas, Capt. To pay annual levy on 14 tytheables to Mr Jno Cox. 24th
  Oct 1653. p 93
Brooks, Mr Nich. See entry Jno Carter. 6 Oct 1653. p 79
Brooks, Thos. See entry David Fox. 6 Aug 1652. p 2
Brooks, Tho. and Mary Arundell. Summoned for "Incentineurie" (arson).
  To have "6 stripes on the bare shoulders with a whip". 6 Oct 1652.
  p 17
Browne, Eliza: Headright of Alex Portus. 7 Aug 1654. p 151
Brown, Fra: To pay annual levy on 3 tytheables to Mr Rd Perrot. 24th
  Oct 1653. p 93
  To be pd from Co levy for 1 wolf. 6 Feb 1654/5. p 173
  To pay levy on 3 tytheables to Mr Rd Perrott. 6 Feb 1654/5. p 174
  Binds himself to pay Wm Clapham Senior 1294 lb tobo 10th Oct next.
  Wit: Rice Jones. George Raules. 6 June 1655. p 195
  To pay levy on 3 tytheables to Abra Weekes. 7 Dec 1655. p 237
Brownrigge, Chesto. Wit Lambertson to Wm's son. 31 Jan 1653/4. p 136
Bruce, Walter. Atty of Ever Petterson. 22 Oct 1652. p 39
Bryan, the Widow. To have 1000 lb tobo for herself and 5 small children
  and Major Jno Carter who has undertaken this in her behalf to be
  pd at next levy. 6 Feb 1654/5. p 172
  The County to pay Major Jo Carter 1000 lb tobo for goods delivered
  to her. 7 Dec 1655. p 233
Bryan, Robt. Pd 100 lb tobo from Co levy for a wolf. 10 Jan 1652/3.
  p 29
  To pay annual levy on 2 tytheables to Mr Jas Bagnall. 24 Oct 1653.
  p 94

Bryan, Robt. To pay levy on one tytheable to Mr Ja Bagnell. 6 Febry 1654/5. p 174

Bryer, Geo: Probate to him of will of Tho Meads, deceased. The estate to be appraised by Am'br Meader, GFran: Gower, Toby Hurst and Tho Robinson. Mr Wm Underwood to admr the oath. 6 June 1655. p 197

Buck, Anthony. Wit Smith-Fauntleroy of Nansemum. See entry Toby Smith. 29 Sept 1647. pp 81-2

Buller, Wm. Headright of Sill Thatcher. 6 Aug 1655. p 208

Bunbridge, Tho. Headright of Mr Toby Smith. 7 Aug 1654. p 151

Bunch, Jno. To give evidence regarding Toby Horton who loaned guns to Indians. 6 June 1654. p 146

    Sub'p on behalf of the Lord Protector agst Toby Horton, and fail- to appear through contempt. Fined 200 lb tobo. 7 Aug. 1654. p 152

Burbage, Col Tho. One of the appraisors of the estate of Epaph: Lawson dec'd. 2 June 1652. p 10

Burbadge, Tho of Virginia, merchant, sells David Fox of Rappa:, planter, 1400 acres taken up by Capt Daniell Gookin 4 Nov 1642 and sold by him to Burbadge. Wit: Ri: Bennett, W Claiborne. 5 June 1652. p 14

Burbage, Col Tho. Assigns a servant to Jno Meriman (the servant formerly assigned to Burbage by Will Buttler) 10 Apl 1653. p 46

Burbadge, Coll. Dif betw Jno Robinson and Wm Sharpe and other of his servants to next Court. 6 Oct 1654. p 163

Burbage, Col Tho. Deceased. His widow married Capt Tho Streator who is sued by Rev Phillip Mallory guardian of Tho Oldis. 17 Mar 1657/8. Northumberland County Records Vol.15, p 4

Burgess, Ann. Headright of Toby Smith. 6 Oct 1652. p 16

Burket, Jno. Headright of Robt Tomlyn. 6 Oct 1653. p 78

Burne, Jno. Headright of Nich Feyman (or Fepman). 6 Feb 1653/4. p 139

Burnham, Mr. Rowland.

He and Capt Townsend sold 6 negroes to Sir Hen Chicheley. 10 Jan 1652/3. p 27

Gives John Wealch a heifer. 6 Apl 1653. p 45

See entry 'Muster'. 8 Aug 1653. p 65

Dif betw him and Jno Pedro to next Court. In interim Mr Jo Paine and Nick Feyman to view the work done by Pedro and give their opinion. 6 Oct 1653. p 77

To pay annual levy on 11 tytheables to Mr Rd Perrot. 24 Oct 1653. p 93.

To be pd 400 lb tobo by Jno Pedro for failing in meeting building agreement. 8 Dec 1653. p 96

See entry Sir Henry Chicheley. 18 Apl 1654. p 129

Wit: deed Nicholls to Jonson. 25 Apl 1653. p 157

To pay levy on 12 tytheables to Mr Rich Perrot. 6 Feb 1654/5. p 174

To appraise the estate of Capt Wm Brocas decd. 7 May 1655. p 189

Signs inventory of Capt Wm Brocas' estate. 14 May 1655. p 202

Burnhams Creek adjs land of Robt Chowninge, Tho Keds, etc. 16 Apl 1655. p 219

To pay levy on 12 tytheables to Abra Weekes. 7 Dec 1655. p 237

Burrows, Tho. To pay annual levy on 2 tytheables to Mr Tho Brice.
   24 Oct 1653. p 91

Burroughs. Tho. Buys 300 acres from Hen Hackary. This land was
   patented 1 Sept 1651 by Hackery and sold by Burroughs to Jno
   Edwards 16 June 1653. p 148. (This entry not quite clear to
   me - the above abstract the best I can make of it. B.F.)

Burton, Robt. Admitted guardian for Jo Johnson and his brothers and
   sisters. 7 Dec 1655. p 231

Burton, Sam: To pay levy on 1 tytheable to Abra Weeks. 7 Dec 1655.
   p 237

Bushrod, Tho: Wit: P of A from Jno Custise of Northampton Co (Va.)
   to Cuth: Potter. 26 July 1653. p 88
   In suit betw him and Vincent Stanford, Jo Meredith's bill for
   450 lb tobo in Stanford's hands, to be delivered to Bushrod, it
   belonging to him. 7 Dec 1655. p 231

Butterworth, Judeth. Wit: P of A Lea to Sheares (London). 20 Sept
   1649. p 5

Buttler, Will. "I doe by these presents confess that John Snooke
   did come into the Country for ten yeares only the indentures
   is lost this I doe testify", "and for the same yeares I assign
   him to Coll Burbage per me Will Butler". Wit: Charles Rawlins.
   Tho Burbage assigns Snooke to John Meriman 7 March 1652/3. "The
   terme of ten yeares I John Snooke doe acknowledge that I came
   over for the 28th of 7ber 1652   John Snooke". Recorded 10th
   April 1653. p 46

Butts, Ja: Ordered to pay Wm Clapham Senr a debt of 750 lb tobo. 6th
   Oct 1653. p 79

Buts, James. Order to Mr Andrew Gilson "To pay James Buts debt upon
   the Burghes' bill" from the levy. 24 Oct 1653. p 94

Butt, Ja: Wit deed Edwards to Ball. 31 Dec 1653. p 149

Byram, Jno. Wit: P of A dated 14 Jan 1650/51 Harris to Astell. See
   entry Hen: Monford as of 12 Aug 1650. p 83

Cable, John. Certificate for land for transportation of Rawleigh
   Travers. 6 Oct 1653. p 79
   To pay levy on 1 tytheable to Mr Ja Bagnell. 6 Feb 1654/5.
   p 174

Carter, Hen: Headright of Mr Andrew Gilson. 6 Oct 1654. p 162

Carter, Honorfit. Headright of Capt Hen Fleet. 24 Oct 1653. p 89

Carter, Major John. Numerous entries to follow.

Carter, Mr Jno. By his atty, Wm Clapham Jr, petitions to have
   administration of estate of Epaphro: Lawson deceased to secure
   debt of 7067 lb tobo. This granted, he to deliver the balance
   to Domino Theriott. 10 Jan 1652/3. p 23

Carter, Jno. His land adj Epa Lawson. 3 Sept 1649. p 33

Carter, Mr Jno. Named as admr in will of Epa: Lawson. 31 March 1652.
   p 34

Carter, Major Jno. Justice. 6 Aug 1653. p 61
To be pd debts from Epa Lawson's estate. See entry Robt Mascall.
6 Aug 1653. p 62
As Justice reproves Rd Denham. See entry Capt Tho Hackett. 8th
Aug 1653. p 63
See entry 'Muster'. 8 Aug 1653. p 65
Justice. 6 Oct 1653
To be pd 2000 lb tobo from this year's levy, due to him as Admr
of Epa Lawson dec'd, for his burgesses charge for 1652. 6 Oct
1653. p 79
An attachment to Maj Jno Carter at the suit of Michaell Mart-
land for L 4. Sterling for goods imported into this Country,
which debt is in the hands of Abra Moone and is due from him
to Mr Nich Brooks and is returnable to next Court, provided
the said Brooks have 8 days notice. 6 Oct 1653. p 79
Witness to Smith - Fantleroy transaction on 10 Sept 1653. See
Toby Smith entry dated 29 Sept 1647. pp 81-2
To pay annual levy on 12 tytheables to Mr Row Lawson. 24th Oct
1653. p 90
In list of County expenses to be pd from levy "To pay Maj'r
John Carter due by order of Court" 1090 lb tobo. 24 Oct 1653.
p 90. Also in list of County expenses "To Major Jo: Carter
per ord for Mr Lawrence charges Ao 1651 1090 lb tobo". 24th
Oct 1653. p 95
In behalf of Toby Smith sells Gyles Webb 1081 acres of land.
6 Feb 1653/4. p 128
To be pd 1276 lb tobo 10 Oct next by Walter Herd. 1st April
1657. (This item is out of order in the records. The date is
as shown) p 130.
Justice. 16 May 1654. p 131
Is owed 12850 lb tobo to be pd 10 Nov next by Thomas Carter.
1st June 1654. p 135
Justice. 6 Feb 1653/4. p 137
Has judgt agt Tho Roots 750 lb tobo. 6 Feb 1653/4. p 139
In reagrd to Edmonds estate. See entry Edwin Conaway. 6th Apl
1654. p 140
Justice. 7 March 1653/4. p 142
Justice. 6 June 1654. p 144
Delivers to Wm Neesam and John Meriman a bill of Capt More
Fantleroy of 3500 lb tobo for paymt of their accounts due from
estate of Epa: Lawson dec'd. etc. 6 June 1654. p 145
See entry Edw Boswell. 6 June 1654. p 146
Justice. 7 Aug 1654. p 151
Justice. 6 Oct 1654. p 162
Pd 30 lb tobo for hire of men to guard the house of Marga:
Grimes "on the Death of the Indian". 6 Oct 1654. p 163
Justice. 6 Feb 1654/5. p 171
Advanced the widow Bryan 1000 lb tobo to aid her and her
children. 6 Feb 1654/5. p 172

Carter, Major Jno. To collect levy for 34 persons incl 12 tytheables
of his own family. 6 Feb 1654/5. p 174
His land abt 8 miles up the Rappa. See entry Wm Clapham Jr. 12
July 1654. p 188
Justice. 6 June 1655. p 196
Has settled in full all a/cs as admr of est of Epa: Lawson, decd.
6 June 1655. p 199
To build Court House at Corotomen. 6 June 1655. p 201
Justice. 25 Oct 1655. p 210
His servt David Miles to be whipped for threatening to strike
him with a hoe. 25 Oct 1655. p 213
Entry all but illegible. Appointed "to be the Cheef Offiser"
for some matter regarding ships and their cargoes in Lancaster
Co. 25 Oct 1655. p 214
Mortgage. See entry Tho Carter. 18 Sept 1655. p 228
The County to pay him 1000 lb tobo for goods delivered to the
widow Bryan. Also 600 lb tobo "for nayles for the lower Court
house". 7 Dec 1655. p 233
To receive payment for levy on 59 tytheables as follows:

Major Jo: Carters plantations on both sides	21
Mr Tho Carter	4
Mr Marsh	4
Sir Henry Chicheley Knt	29
Henry Rie	1

7th Dec 1655. p 234
Carter, Susana. Headright of Mr Tho Carter. 6 Feb 1654/5. p 172
Carter, Tho. Bond to pay him 1095 lb tobo by Tho Seamor. 16 March
1652/3. p 47
To pay levy on 7 tytheables to Mr Row Lawson. 24 Oct 1653. p 90
Wit: mortgage Nichols to Linell. 30 Nov 1653. p 105
Is indebted to John Carter 12850 lb tobo to be pd 10 Nov next
"at my now Dwelling house". Wit: Geo Marsh. 1 June 1654. p 135
To be pd 690 lb tobo by exor of Epa Lawson. 6 Feb 1653/4. p 137
Certificate for land for transportation of 7 persons: Susana
Carter, Wm Shirt, Mary Smyth, An Hughs, Jos Maxy, Mark Smyth,
Edw Lunce. 6 Feb 1654/5. p 172
To pay levy on 4 tytheables to Major Jno Carter. 6 Feb 1654/5.
p 174
Wit: deed of Tho Hackett. 25 Oct 1655. p 226
Promises to pay Jno Carter L 100. First paymt to be 10 June
1657. Security the plantation formerly belonging to Capt Wm
Brocas Esq. Wit: Diana Skipwith, Anne Ebbesonn. Recorded 10
Oct. 1655. p 228
To pay levy on 4 tytheables to Majr Jo: Carter. 7 Dec 1655.
p 234
Catten, Wm. (Cotton ?). Arrested by Wm Wraughton for debt of 260 lb
tobo. Failing to appear a judgmt agst Rice Jones his security.
6 June 1654. p 146

Catton, Wm. (name practically illegible and subject to correction)
Judgmt to him agt Edward Bradshaw and also Wm Breian for - 1b
tobo. 6 Aug 1655. p 208
Catton, Will. To be pd 150 lb tobo from County levy by Mr Bagnall
for a wolf's head. 7 Dec 1655. p 236
Cattlett, Jno, Wit Coniers to Davis. 16 Oct 1652. p 49
Wit: Davis to Nickolls. 27 March 1653. p 50
Wit: Deed Lewis to Willis and Watkins. 7 Aug 1654. p 155
To collect levy on 23 tytheables incl 5 of his own family. 6th
Feb 1654/5. p 174
Wit: assignmt of land Lucas to Hawkins. 3 Feb 1654/5. p 218
Wit: assignmt of 600 acres Lucas to Hawkings. 3 Feb 1654/5.
p 220
His land on S side Rappa adjs a patent of Tho Lucas. 7 August
165- (blotted, prior to 1654 P p 220
Chambers, Robt. decd. His estate to be appraised by Mr Rich Lawson
and Mr Rich Colman. 6 Apl 1654. p 140
Prob of his will to Jno Woir. 6 Apl 1654. p 141
Chambers, Robt. Appears twice as headright of Jno Weir. 6 Oct 1654.
p 162
Chambers, Robt. dec'd. His exor Jno Weir. 6 Oct 1654. p 162
His exor, Jno Weir, sues Sil Thatcher for use of sloop from
James River. 6 Aug 1655. p 209
Chatton, Tho: Headright of Abra Weeks. 6 Oct 1653. p 77
Chester, An: Headright of Capt More Fantleroy. 1 July 1652. p 1.
Chew, Sam: Wit P of A Jno Jefrys of London to Col Rd Lee. 7th Feb
1652/3. p 112
Chicheley, the ladie Agatha gives her niece, Eltonhead the daughter
of Edwin Conaway, a black cow called Thacker. If she die the
cow to "my sister Martha the wife of the said Edwin Conaway".
Wit: Cuth Potter. John x Pig. 7 May 1653. p 68
Chicheley. Note: We were always told that the pronunciation of this
old English name was 'Chesley' and that the vulgar pronounced
it 'Chisley'. It appears in these records as Chicheley, Chisley
and as Chichley.
Chisley, Sir Henry. Certificate for importing 16 persons. 10th Jan.
1652/3. p 27
Chicholey, Sir Hen. Wit receipt Conway to Brocas. 15 May 1653. p 69
Chisley, Sr Hen: To pay annual levy on 17 tytheables to Mr John
Cox. (This item shows the largest number of tytheables in the
County as of that date). 24 Oct 1653. p 93
Chisley, Sir Hen: Reference to a calf at his plantation in Rappa:
River belonging to Abra: Moone. 18 Oct 1653. p 103
Chicheley, Sir Henry of Rappa in the County of Lancaster, Knt., and
Dame Agatha his wife and late widow of Col Ralph Wormley Esq.
That Dame Agatha in her widowhood made 2 deeds. In one dated
30 May 1652, she gave her two sons, William and Ralph Wormley,
several lands, personal property, etc., with the provision if
either die before 21, his part to the survivor. Capt Wm Brocas,

(see next page)

Chicheley, Sir Henry (continued)
    Mr Wm Eltonhead and Mr Row: Burnham trustees. And further the
    said Wm Wormley is since dead and his estate belongs to his
    brother Ralph Wormley and is now held by the following trustees:
    Sir Hen: Chicheley Knt., Capt Wm Brocas Esqr, Edw Digs Esqr,
    Mr Wm Eltonhead and Mr Row: Burnham. Wit: Alex Cook, cler.
    Hen Waldron, Roger Marshall. 18 Apl 1654. p 129. Further
    entries to same effect with same names. p 129.
Chicheley, Sir Hen. Land transaction. See entry Capt Wm Brocas. 28th
    January 1653. p 133
Chisley, Sir Henry. A Court held at his house. 7 March 1653/4. p 140
Chisley, Sir Hen: Judgt to him agst est of Capt Da: How. 7 March
    1653/4. p 142
Chichley, Sir Hen: Dif betw him and Abra Moone to next Court. 6th
    Feb 1654/5. p 173
Chichley, Sir Hen. To pay levy on 24 tytheables to Mr. Jno Cox. 6th
    Feb 1654/5. p 174
Chicheley, Sir Hen: see entry Capt Wm Brocas, Esqr, decd. 7th May
    1655. p 189
Chicheley, Sir Hen: Estate made over to him by Capt Wm Brocas for
    use of Mrs Eleanor Brocas. 17 Nov 1652. p 190
Chicheley, Sir Henry. To pay levy on 29 tytheables to Major Jo: Carter
    7 Dec 1655. p 234
Chowninge, Robt. His land on Burnham's Creek adjs Tho Ked's, etc.
    16 Apl 1655. p 219
Church. "next meeting when there shall be a sermon". See entry David
    Fox. 6 Aug 1652. p 2
    See entry Rev. Alexander Cooke. 6 Oct 1652. p 15
    See entry Mr Tho Brice. 6 Apl 1653. p 44
    Two churches. See entry Mrs Joane Thomas. 9 Dec 1653. p 99
Clapham, Wm. Com of admr of est of Wm Foote decd to him for debt
    of 700 lb tobo. 10 Jan 1652/3. p 23
Clapham, Wm. Half of 300 acres sold by him to Tho Powell and John
    Paine belongs to Charles Snead, Paine having sold his half to
    Snead. 5 Dec 1652. p 48
Clapham, Wm. vs Toby Horton to next Court. 6 Aug 1655. p 209
Clapham, Wm. His land on Corotomen River adj Thos Hackett. 25 Oct
    1655. p 226
Clapham, Wm. Sells Capt Henry Fleet 700 acres which formerly was
    sold by Mr Richd Bennett Esqr to Ephroditus Lawson and by
    Lawson sold to Clapham. The 700 acres is on a neck of land
    part of which Clapham sold Mr Stevens and a parcel of which
    was leased to Saml Sloper. Sloper to have peaceable possession
    the term of his lease. Dated the last day of June 1655.
    Wit: Hough Brent. Tho Allenson. Recorded 25 Oct 1655. p 229
Clappam, Wm. Dif betw him and Jno Walton to next Court. 7th Dec.
    1655. p 232
Clapham, Wm Jr., who married the relict of Epaphroditas Lawson to
    have interest in a mortgage to Richd Bennett Esqr from Lawson.
    6 Oct 1652. p 16

Clapham, Wm Jr. Atty of Mr Jno Carter. 10 Jan 1652/3. p 23
    See entry Rd Bennett. 12 Sept 1652. p 31
    Letter from Ri Bennett to Mr Toby Smith concerning him. 12 Sept
    1652. p 32
    Com of admr to him on estate of Wm Kitchin decd. 6 Apl 1653.
    p 43
    Judgt to him agt Jno Phillips for amt due from Thos Ro-. 6 Apl
    1653. p 44
    Sued by Robt Mascall. See involved entry in his name. 6 August
    1653. p 62
    To pay levy on 6 tytheables to Mr Row Lawson. 24 Oct 1653. p 90
    His land on W side Corotomen. Adjs Wm Wraughton. 29 Nov 1652.
    p 116.
    As exor of Mr Epa Lawson is ordered to pay debt of 690 lb tobo
    to Mr Tho Carter. 6 Feb 1653/4. p 137
    Security for Jno Meredith and Walter Herd admrs of Mrs Frances
    Edmonds decd. 7 March 1653/4. p 142
    Impleaded Marg Grimes widow for debt of 1 hhd tobo due from Wm
    Downman dec'd. She ordered to settle the a/c which has been
    partly pd. 6 June 1654. p 144
    Certificate of land for transportation of 7 persons: Jno Cooke,
    Fran Sewell, Marga Mallo:, Eliz Cornish, Jno Cornish, Sara
    Cornish, X'per Harford. 6 June 1654. p 145
    Judgt agst Marg: Grimes widow for 130 lb tobo. 6 June 1654.
    p 146
    Attorney of Mr Wm Haier. 7 Aug 1654. p 151
    Is pd 30 lb tobo for hire of men to guard Marga: Grimes' house.
    6 Oct 1654. p 163
    To pay levy on 7 tytheables to Major Jno Carter. 6 Feb 1654/5.
    p 174
    Sells to Jno Steephenson 700 acres in Rappa about 8 miles up,
    as by patent dated 3 Sept, being a neck adj Slaughters Creek
    and adj Maj Jno Carter. Wit: Tho Madestard. Geo Goldsmith.
    Dower rights relinq by Eliza x Clapham. 12 July 1654. p 188
    His a/c included in settlement of Lawson estate. 20 Jan 1655/6.
    p 192
    Appears as attorney of Jas Hannum in suit for 2500 lb tobo vs
    J Philips for nonappearance of Tobyas Horton. 6 June 1655. p 196
    His name appears in an illegible entry concerning market places.
    25 Oct 1655. p 214
    Sued by Jno Cox is ordered to pay him 627 lb tobo. 7 Dec 1655.
    p 232
Clapham, William, Senior.
    Appointed Constable on North side of Rappahannock River. He to
    repair to the next Com'r of the Quorum that he shall live by,
    Mr. Tho Brice. 6 Aug 1652. p 3
    Certificate for land for importing 2 persons, Salter Knight
    and Thomas Orange. 6 Oct 1652. p 15

Clapham, Wm. Senior. Judgt agt him as security for Wm Thatcher who
    was arrested at suit of Elias Edmonds and did not appear. 6th
    April 1653. p 43
    To be pd 750 lb tobo by Ja: Butts. 6 Oct 1653. p 79
    Judgt agt Jno Phillips 660 lb tobo if Tho Roots fails to appear
    at next Court. 6 Oct 1653. p 79
    To be pd 930 lb tobo by Enock Hauker. 6 Oct 1653. p 80
    To pay levy on 5 tytheables to Mr Row Lawson. 24 Oct 1653. p 90
    To appraise the estate of Elias Edmonds dec'd. 6 June 1654.
    p 144
    To be pd 558 lb tobo from est of Elias Edmonds decd. 6 June 1654.
    p 145
    "Mr Clapham Senior" to collect levy on 15 tytheables including
    5 tytheables of his own family. 6 Feb 1654/5. p 174
    To be pd 1294 lb tobo 10 Oct next by Francis Browne. 6 June
    1655. p 195
    To pay levy to V Stanford. 7 Dec 1655. p 235
Clarke, Arther. Order that Mr David Fox deliver all cattle belong-
    ing to him. 25 Oct 1655. p 211
Clarke, Daniell "of the Iland of Virginia", planter. Power of Atty
    from Mrs Bridgett Kempe to him. 9 Sept 1651. p 57
Clark, Philip. Headright of Sill Thatcher. 6 Aug 1655. p 208
Clarke see Clearke.
Clay, Columbus. Headright of Geo Taylor. 6 Oct 1654. p 162
Clayborne, William. This well known person appears as Claiborne, etc.
    Wit: bond Rice Jones to Rd Bennett. 7 June 1652. p 6
    Wit: deed Rd Bennett to Rice Jones. 7 June 1652. p 8
    Wit: deed Burbage to Fox. 5 June 1652. p 14
    Wit: deed Bennett to Dedman. 4 June 1652. p 21
    Wit: deed Bennett to Jackman. 4 June 1652. p 22
Clayborne, Coll Wm Esq. Nonsuited in action agst Elizabeth relict
    of John Taylor. 6 Apl 1653. p 43
Clayborne, Wm. Wit: Bennett to Loes. 4 June 1652. p 46
    To agree for Northumberland Co regarding the Ferry. See entry
    Ferry. 9 Dec 1653. p 101
    Signs patent with Ri Bennett to Tho Lucas. 7 June 1652. p 221
Clearke, Arth: Son in law to Mr Da: Fox petitions for a guardian
    and no longer to remain in tuition of his father in law, he
    being of sufficient age. Mr Tho Griffin appointed his guardian.
    Mr Fox to surrender the orphan's estate. 6 June 1655. p 200
Cleashe, Patrick. Headright of Mr Row Lawson. 6 Feb 1654/5. p 172
Clouda, Jno. Headright of Mr Toby Smith. 7 Aug 1654. p 151
Cloyd, Angus. Headright of Geo Taylor. 6 Oct 1654. p 162
Cookman, Wm. Headright of Wm Tigner. 6 Apl 1653. p 43
Coggan, Tho. Wit assignmt of land by Jno Meriman. 9 Sept 1654. p 183
Cole, Alice the wife of Fra: Cole gives a calf to Alice daughter of
    Luke Davies. 10 Feb 1653/4. p 117
Cole, Mr. To pay annual levy on 3 tytheables to Mr Rd Perrot. 24th
    Oct 1653. p 93

Cole, Mr. To pay levy for 3 tytheables to Abra Weekes. 7 Dec 1655.
    p 237
Cole, Fra: To pay levy on 5 tytheables to Mr Rd Perrott. 6th Feby
    1654/5. p 174
Coale, Mr Fra: To appraise estate of Capt Wm Brocas decd. 7th May
    1655. p 189
Coales, Mr Fra: Reference to his plantation. See entry Markets. 6th
    June 1655, p 201
Coale, Fra. Signs inventory of Capt Wm Brocas' estate. 14 May 1655.
    p 202
Cole, Rd. Wit: Pedro and Davis to White and Welch. 23 May 1652. p 45
    Wit: deed Boswell to Davies and Pedro. 18 May 1653. p 118
    Wit: deed Hagett to Potter. 30 Oct 1654. p 178
Coleman, Richd. Patent. 320 acres on N. side Rappahannock River near
    land of Wm Newsome and land now in possession of Rice Jones. No
    date shown. The patent issued by Sir Wm Berkeley. Coleman
    assigns his right in the land to Robt Mascall. Also no date.
    Wit by Tho Roots. Rice Jones.   Mascall assigns his right in
    the land to Rice Jones. Wit: Edwin Conaway. John Walker. 28th
    Feb 1652/3.   Rice Jones assigns his right in the land to
    Howell Powell and Geo Harris. Wit: Edwin Conaway. John Walker.
    28th Feb 1652/3.   Howell Powell assigns his right in the land
    to Charles Sneade. Wit: Geo Beach. 5 March 1652/3. Recorded 6
    April 1653. pp 54-5
Coleman, Richard. "8ber 18th Richard Coleman hath ordered a Caveat
    for an Adminstracon of his brother in Law Robt Mascalls Estate".
    1653. p 80
Coleman, Rich. To pay levy on 2 tytheables to Mr Andrew Gilson. 24
    Oct 1653. p 94
Colman, Mr Rich: to appraise estate of Robt Chambers decd. 6 April
    1654. p 140
Colman, Rich. Grant of 600 acres in "the fresh" on South side of
    Rappa. Adjs land of Geo Mosleye. 14 Sept 1650.   He sells the
    land for 4000 lb tobo to Wm Neale and Jno Vauss. Wit: Thomas -
    (the last name of this witness is omitted from record). John
    Weir. 4 June 1655. p 206
Colinge, Eliz. Headright of Capt Hen Fleete. 24 Oct 1653. p 89
Collin, Wm. (?). Headright of Edwin Conway. 6 Aug 1653. p 62
Collins, Ann. Headright of Jno Weir. 6 Oct 1654. p 162
Collins, Geo. A long and tedious suit betw him as pltf and Samuel
    Perry as deft. Perry ordered to pay him 2700 lb tobo. 7 Dec.
    1655. p 231
Colloins, Eliz. Difficult to read. May be incorrect. Headright of
    Da: Felps. 6 Feb 1653/4. p 139
Coniers, Denis. His land adjs that sold by Pedro and Davis to White
    and Welch. 23 May 1652. p 45
Coniers, Den'is. planter. Sells Evan Davis 100 acres patented 12th
    Feb 1651/2, half a mile above Boswell's plantation, etc. Wit:
    John Cattlett. 16 Oct 1652. p 49

Coniers, Denis. Wit: Davis to Nickolls. 27 Mar 1653. p 50

Coniers, Denis. Letter to Mr Smith to acknowledge sale of land to
    Evan Davis. Dated "From Capt Brocas his house this 26th of
    March 1653". Signed Denis Coniers. p 50

Coniers, Denis. His land on Sunderland Creek. 5 March 1651/2. p 118
    His land on S side Rappa. See entry Capt Wm Brocas. 18th Nov
    1653. p 133
    His land on Sunderland Creek adj Evan Davies and opp Henry
    Nicholls. 29 July 1652. p 157
    To pay levy on 2 tytheables to Mr Tho Bourne. 6 Feb 1654/5.
    p 174.
    To pay levy on 3 tytheables to Mr Kempe. 7 Dec 1655. p 239

Constables for this year. John Gillett, Edw Boswell, Teage Floyne.
    6 April 1653. p 44

Conway, Edwin. His name is almost invariably spelled 'Conaway' in
    this order book.
    Certificate 100 acres for importing 2 persons. Alice Ellis, Ann
    Roberts. 6 Oct 1652. p 15
    Dif betw him and Mary Doney to next Court. 6 Oct 1652. p 16
    Wit deed Jackman to Edgecomb. 29 Dec 1652. p 19
    Suit agst him by Antho and Mary Doney dismissed, they not
    appearing. 10 Jan 1652/3. p 25
    Wit: Jones to Powell. 8 Jan 1652. p 51
    Wit: Jones to Powell. 22 Jan 1652/3. p 53
    Wit: Mascall to Rice Jones. Also Rice Jones to Powell and
    Harris. 28 Feb 1652/3. pp 54-5
    Certificate for importing 2 persons. Wm Collin, Edward Ben'ett.
    6 August 1653. p 62
    Registers marks for cattle. For Edwin Conaway, Edwin Conaway
    Junir (sic) and Eltonhead Conaway. 10 Aug 1653. p 68
    Receipt for a cow from Mrs Elnor Brocas "by the apointmt of my
    sister Fenwick in the time of her widowhood" for use of his dau
    Eltonhead, it being "a Gift from her Aunt Fenwick". Wit: Hen
    Chicheley. Cuth Potter. 15 May 1653. p 69
    Wit deed Battersby to Newsam and Pinn. See entry Newsam et als.
    21 March 1652. p 70
    To pay levy on 5 tytheables to Mr Row Lawson. 24 Oct 1653. p 90
    To be pd 100 lb tobo by Jas Yates assigned from Tho Roots. 9th
    Dec 1653. p 99
    He and Martha Conaway wit lease Nicholls to Boyer. 22 Dec 1652.
    p 114
    Wit receipt Potter to Grimes. 30 Nov 1653. p 117
    Wit pre-nuptial agreemt Roots and Attawell. 14 Oct 1653. p 121
    By letter requests reference to next Court to be held at Maj:
    John Carter's house, for a hearing on the will of Elias Edmonds
    dec'd. Whereas Jo Meredith and Walter Hurd, at a Court at the
    house of Sir Henry Chicheley 7 March 1653/4 procured admr on
    the estate of Fra: Edmonds relict of the sd Elyas, etc. The
    matter is referred to the next Court. 6 April 1654. p 140

Conway, Edwin. (or Conaway)
    Sued by Jno Jeffryes for L 19. 16. Sterling. Does not appear.
    6 April 1654. p 141
    To appraise the estate of Elias Edmonds decd. 6 June 1654. p 144
    To appraise the estate of Wm Downman decd. 6 June 1654. p 145
    His land on E side Corotomen River, adjs Capt Tho Hackett and
    land of Jno Nicolls. 29 Nov 1652. p 165
    In dif with Abra Moone atty of Jno Jefferyes. 6 Feb 1654/5.
    p 173
    To pay levy on 4 tytheables to Mr Clapham senior. 6 Feb 1654/5.
    p 174
    Wit deed Borough to Hopkins. 5 Feb 1654/5. p 180
    Wit Brocas to Chicheley. 17 Nov 1652. p 190
    To pay levy on 4 tytheables to Wm Leech. 7 Dec 1655. p 236
Conaway, Martha. Wit assignmt Brocas to Chicheley. 28 Jan 1653/4.
    p 133
Conway family detail. See entry "the ladie Agatha Chicheley". 7th
    May 1653. p 68
Cooke, Rev. Alexander. "Mr Alexander Cooke cler". His proposition
    to the Court approved. Also by all the inhabitants present.
    Certificate to be sent to him. 6 Oct 1652. p 15.
Cooke, Rev. Alexander. A lengthy, courteous but positive letter to
    the Commissioners giving terms. Double tythes the first year,
    etc., "for my removeall from Ja: River into this County". Will
    come "about the 25th of March next ensueinge and there shall
    be readie to officiate in v't 2 places of the river yu your-
    selves shall Judge convenient". A boat to be sent for his re-
    moval. Signed Alex Cooke. Dated "From Mr Foxes house September
    26th 1652". Recorded 9 Oct 1652. pp 41-2
Cooke, Alex, Clerk. Wit deed of gift Fantleroy to Griffin. 22 Sept
    1653. p 74.   Also wit deed Fantleroy to Griffin. 22 Sept 1653.
    p 75
    Wit trust transaction Chicheley for Wormeley. 18 Apl 1654. p 129
Cooke, Jno. Servt to Epa Lawson. 13 Apl 1651. p 9
    Was servt to Epa Lawson. To serve 3 yrs. 2 June 1652. p 10
    Headright of Wm Clapham Jr. 6 June 1654. p 145
Cooke, Mar't. Headright of Mr Ja: Bagnall. 6 Aug 1655. p 208
Cooper, Danl. Headright of Mr Row Lawson. 6 Feb 1654/5. p 172
Cooper, Richerd. Headright of Mr Tho. Hawkins. 6 Aug 1655. p 208
Cooper, Sam. Wit P of A Jno Jefrys of London to Col Rd Lee. 7 Feb
    1652/3. p 112
Cooper, Tho. To pay levy on 2 tytheables to Mr Felson. 7 Dec 1655.
    p 238
    To pay levy on 1 tytheable to Da Fox. 7 Dec 1655. p 238
Cornelis, Jno. Petitions by his atty Jno Meriman for 1095 lb tobo
    due from estate of Epa Lawson, decd. 10 Jan 1652/3. p 24
Cornish, Elizabeth, John and Sara. Headrights of Wm Clapham Jr. 6th
    June 1654. p 145
Corrithes, John. Headright of Mr Tho Hawkins. 6 Aug 1655. p 208

Corslan, Ann. Headright of David Fox. 6 Oct 1652. p 15

Cotton see Catton.

Coucreret, Jeremias. Wit: P of A Montfort to Moseley. 12th August 1650 (date doubtful) p 83

Coulstone, Frances. Headright of Wm Jonson. 6 Oct 1652. p 15

Coupland, Wm. see Copland and Coopland.

Coopland, Wm. carpenter. Buys 537 acres from Danl and Eliz Welsh. 6 June 1655. p 194

Copland, Wm. Order to him for 1000 lb tobo in suit vs J Phillips for nonappearance of Abra Moone. 6 June 1655. p 196

Coupland, Wm. Judgmt confessed to him by Abra Moone for 2000 lb tobo with 1 yr interest. 6 Aug 1655. p 208

Copland, Wm. (this name also appears in the entry as Coopland) Says Mr Kempe owes him 270 lb tobo. Mr Tho Greefieth and Mr Kemp to pay the costs of the suit. 25 Oct 1655. p 211

Copeland, Wm. Security for Robt Burton guardian of Jo Johnson and his brothers and sisters. 7 Dec 1655. p 231

Court House. Order for survey of land at Corotomen for a Court house. Also "likewise for the whole booke of acts in force". 6 Febry 1654/5. p 172

Major Jno Carter has undertaken to build the Court house at Corotomen. Mr Wm Underwood to build the like on the land adj his house. 6 June 1655. p 2ol

See entry Wm Wraton. 6 June 1655. p 201

Court house to be built by Wm Neasham on land formerly Downmans. 25 Oct 1655. p 212

Order that a Court House for the upper part of the County be erected at Mr Underwood's last June. Now ordered that a market be kept there. The County is indebted 10000 lb tobo for the building of 2 Court Houses. 7 Dec 1655. p 233

Major Jno Carter to be pd 600 lb tobo "for nayles for the lower Court House". 7 Dec 1655. p 233

Payment of 1979 lb tobo made from County levy to Wm Neesham towards building the Court House. 7 Dec 1655. p 236

Willm Neesham in collecting the levy "To detaine in his owne hands towards the building of the Courthouse 2211 lb tobo". 7th Dec. 1655. p 237

The next Court for the upper part of this County to be kept at the house of Mr Underwood 6 Jan: p 239. The next Court for the lower part of the County to be at house of Wm Neesham 6th Feb if the Courthouse is not built by that time. p 240. 7th Dec 1655.

Courtman, Tho. Headright of Danl Welch. 6 Aug 1653. p 62

Cox, Mr John.

Justice. 6 Apl 1653. p 43

See entry 'Muster'. 8 Aug 1653

Admrs of Epa Lawson decd ordered to pay him 595 lb tobo. 6 Oct 1653. p 77

Justice. 6 Oct 1653. p 77

Cox, Mr. John. To collect annual levy for these families, vizt:

Ja Boimer	02
Mr Tigner	05
Mr Cox himselfe	03
Mr Kempe	16
Coll Lee	10
Ca Brocas	14
Mr Moone	05
Sr Hen: Chisley	17
	------
	72 tytheables

24 Oct 1653. p 93

Cox, John. Agreemt with Tho Littlepage regarding a debt due him.
(the debt due Cox). 16 Jan 1653/4. p 104.
Buys 2 cows from Wm Underwood. 26 Nov 1653. p 104
Headright twice of Da: Felps. 6 Feb 1653/4. p 139
Justice. 6 June 1654. p 144
To admr oath to appraisers of est of Rd Lake decd. 6 Oct 1654.
p 162
To collect levy on 86 tytheables incl 4 tytheables of his own
family. 6 Feb 1654/5. p 174
To appear and prove right to administer the estate of Paule
Brewer. If not admr to Wm Jno'son. The est to be appraised by
Cl: Thrush, Jno Bebey and Robt Yonge and Mr And: Gilson to
admr the oath. 6 June 1655. p 201
Justice 25 Oct 1655. p 210
Ordered to pay the estate of Paule Brewer dec'd 232 lb tobo.
25 Oct 1655. p 211
Cox, John of London, now resident in Virginia. See entries Richard
Pettibone. 1 Dec 1655. p 224
Cox, Mr John. Justice. 7 Dec 1655. p 231
In dif betw him and Mr Wm Clapham Jr, Clapham ordered to pay
Cox 627 lb tobo. 7 Dec 1655. p 232
Dif betw him and Tho Boeman to next Court. 7 Dec 1655. p 232
Dif betw him and Mr Tho Breamer to next Court. 7 Dec 1655. p 232
To pay levy on 3 tytheables to Wm Leech. 7 Dec 1655. p 236
Cox, Mr Tho. Justice. 7 March 1653/4. p 142. Possibly this entry is
an error in the original. The person meant may be Mr. John Cox.
Coxe's Creek. On South side of Rappahannock. 27 Oct 1652. p 160
Craford, Jno. Headright of Abra Moone. 7 Aug 1654. p 153
Crispe, Wm. Headright of Mr Tho Hawkins. 6 Aug 1655. p 208
Croscombe, Jas. Sold goods to James Williamson in 1648. See entry
Hen: Montford. 12 Aug 1650. p 83
Crowde, Tho. Headright of Mr Toby Smith. 7 Aug 1654. p 151
Crowded, Thos. Merchant. (Crowder ?). Died while a passenger on Capt
Whitty: ship the Rich: and Ben of London. In his will desired
that Capt John Whitty, Commander of the ship, dispose of his
estate on board and debts due him in Virginia and return all
to his kindred in England as shown in the will. Admr granted
to Capt. John Whittey. 7 March 1653/4. p 142

Cuerzee, Symon. Is owed 40000 lb tobo by Epa Lawson. Richd Bennett,
merchant, stands security. 13 Apl 1651. p 9
His attorney, Rich: Richardson, obtains judgt agst estate of
Epa Lawson for 8431 lb tobo. 8 Dec 1653. p 96
Cullaine, Thach. Headright of Capt Hen Fleet. 24 Oct 1653. p 89
Curtis, Mr. To pay levy on 6 tytheables to Wm Leech. 7 Dec 1655.
p 236
Curtis, Maj Tho. See entry Abra Weeks. 6 Feb 1653/4. p 137
Judgt confessed to him for 500 lb tobo with 2 yrs int by John
Jonson. 6 Oct 1654. p 163
Custise, John of Northampton Co, merchant. P of A. To Cuthbert
Potter to receive from admrs of John Eaton, merchant, dec'd,
accounts due. Wit: Tho: Bushrod. 26 July 1653. p 88. Also see
entry Jno Eaton. 8 Dec 1653. p 97

Dedman, Henry. Bond to Richd Bennett, merchant, 8337 lb tobo. Wit:
Will Jonson. Rich Loes. 4 June 1652. p 4
Buys for 7500 lb tobo, 550 acres on S side Rappa River, from
Richd Bennett merchant. Part of a patent dated 4 Nov 1642. Wit:
W Claiborne. Wm Jonson. Richard Loes. 4 June 1652. p 21
Gave 5 hogs to Ann Jonson dau of Wm Jonson. Now exchanged for
a red cow. 19 Jan 1652/3. p 30
Gives his son Henry a heifer. 19 Jan 1652/3. p 30
Dif betw him and Tho Paine re boundries to next Court. 6 Oct
1653. p 78
To pay annual levy on 3 tytheables to Mr Jas Bagnall. 24 Oct
1653. p 94
Admr of Anth: Nesam dec'd as greatest creditor. 8 Dec 1653.
p 96
With Wm Lynell attaches the estate of Oli Segar. 6 Apl 1654.
p 140
To pay levy on 2 tytheables to Mr Ja Bagnall. 6 Feb 1654/5.
p 174
Deceased. Com of Admr on his estate to Mr Perrott. 6 June 1655.
p 196
Dedman's Creek. See entry 'Muster'. 8 Aug 1653. p 65
Denby, Wm. Fined 700 lb tobo for delivering a gun belonging to
Domine Therriot to an Indian. 6 Oct 1654. p 163
Denhawes, Richard, Elle, William and Susanna, children of Mrs Mary
Hackett. See entry Tho Hackett. 25 Oct 1655. p 226
Denham, Richard. "sun in law to Cap'tt Thomas Hackett". See entry
his name. 8 Aug 1653. p 63
Denham appears in same entry as Denhawes. 25 Oct 1655. p 226
Dennis, David. Headright of V Stanford. 6 June 1655. p 198
Daffer, Mr. To be pd 150 lb tobo from County levy by Mr Da: Fox for
a wolves head. 24 Oct 1653. p 91 (Note: I wonder what on
earth this name actually was ? B.F.)
Dale, Edward. Wit: Herd to Carter. 1 Apl 1657. p 130. This date is
as shown. The item is out of order in the records.

Dale, Edw. Sworn Clerk of this Court. 7 Dec 1655. p 231
> Now Clerk of this Court. To be pd 500 lb tobo from the estate
> of Mr Phillips deceased, former Clerk, for procuring Acts of
> Assemoly for this County. 7 Dec 1655. p 240
> His signature followed by "Cl Cur" (Clerk of the Court). 4th
> Dec 1655. p 241

Dale, Nicho. Late deceased. See involved entry in the name of Chas:
Allen concerning family relationships. 23 Oct 1649. p 48
> His land adj Tho Godwin on S side Rappa. 15 Sept 1651. p 147

Dale's land. Abt 6 miles up Rappa on S side. 10 Feb 1653/4. p 178

Dandridge, Elis. deceased. Left bequest to Rowland, son of Rowland
Lawson prior to 10 Jan 1652/3. p 25

Davids, Em. Wit deed Lewis to Willis and Watkins. 4 Jan 1653/4. p 155

Davis, Evan. He and Jno Pedro sell a neck of land, adj his own land,
to Rd White and Jno Welch. 23 May 1652, p 45
> Buys 100 acres from Den'is Coniers. 16 Oct 1652. p 49
> Buys land from Denis Coniers. See entries his name. "26 March
> 1653". p 50
> In deed shown as 'planter in Virginia'. Sells to Hen: Nickolls
> 150 acres purchased of Denis Coniers. Wit: Jno Cattlett. Denis
> Coniers. Dated 27 Mar 1653. Recorded 10 Apl 1653. p 50
> With Jno Pedro buys land on Sunderland Creek from Edw Boswell
> 16 May 1653, then assigns his interest to Pedro. p 118

Davis, Evan. This name now appears as Davies.
> His land on Sunderland Creek. 5 March 1651/2. p 118
> His land on S side Rappahannock. See entry Capt Wm Brocas. 18th
> Nov 1653. p 133
> Wit deed Nicholls to Jonson. 25 Apl 1653. p 157
> His land on Sunderland Creek adj Denis Coniers and opp Henry
> Nicholls. 29 July 1652. p 157
> To pay levy on 3 tytheables to Mr Rd Perrott. 6 Feb 1654/5.
> p 174
> To view land sold by Moone to Dun. 6 June 1655. p 196
> To pay levy on 6 tytheables to Abra Weekes. 7 Dec 1655. p 237

Davies, Luke. His daughter Alice given a calf by Alice Cole the wife
of Fra: Cole. 10 Feb 1653. p 117
> Wit land assignmt by Jno Meriman. 9 Sept 1654. p 183

Davys, Mr. To pay levy on 2 tytheables to Wm Neesham. 7 Dec 1655.
p 237

Dawson, Richd. To be pd for one wolf. 6 Feb 1654/5. p 173

Dickeson, Walter of Northampton Co. Va. Buys 300 acres from John
Edwards betw 16 June 1653 and 1655. Exact date not shown. p 148
> To pay levy on 6 tytheables to Mr Tho Brice. 6 Feb 1654/5. p 174

Dikeson, Mr. To pay levy on 4 tytheables to Wm Neesham. 7 Dec 1655.
p 237

Digs, Edw Esqr. See entry Sir Hen: Chicheley. 18 Apl 1654. p 129

Diskey, Daniel. Servt to Epa Lawson. 13 Apl 1651. p 9

Doerders, Miner (being Minor Doodes, Doodes Minor or however you
care to have it). Buys 2 cows from Tho Meade. 17th Nov 1653.
p 221.

Dolden, Mary. Headright of Danl Welch. 6 Aug 1653. p 62
Dollinge, Jno. Wit Edwards to Dickeson. Exact date not shown but
    betw 16 June 1653 and 1655. p 148
Doney, Antho: and Mary. Their suit agst Mr Edwin Conway dismissed,
    they not appearing. 10 Jan 1652/3. p 25
Doney, Antho: He and Enoch Hawker have grant of 1000 acres in Lanc.
    Co on N.W. branch of Corotomen. 29 July 1652. p 47
    See entry Jas Yates regarding the death of his servant Math:
    Welbeloved. 6 Aug 1653. p 63
Doney, Mary. Dif betw her and Edwin Conaway to next Court. 6th Oct
    1652. p 16
    She having remained in custody on accusation of Jas Yates to
    be acquitted and released. 6 Oct 1653. p 79
Doodes, Minor. See entry Miner Doerders. 17 Nov 1653. p 221
Dower, Andrew. His a/c incl in settlemt of Epa Lawson's estate. 20th
    Jan 1655/6. p 192
Downham, Wm. Confesses judgt to Jno Sharpe 2000 lb tobo. 10th Jan
    1652/3. p 26 (This is of course Wm Downman. See below)
Downman, Wm. Buys with Edwd Dudley and Ben Powell 300 acres on
    Grymes Creek from Jno Sharpe. See entry Tho Harwood. 6th Feb
    1651/2. p 119
    Deceased. See entry Wm Clapham Jr. 6 June 1654. p 144
    Deceased. Died "very poor and not able to pay the charge of an
    Administracon". Upon petition of John Nicholls on behalf of his
    daughter, the wife and relict of Downman, order that the estate
    be appraised by Capt Tho Hackett and Mr Edwin Conway. 6 June
    1654. p 145
    Quitus est to Jno Nicholls on his estate. 6 Oct 1654. p 164
    A Courthouse to be built on land formerly his. 25 Oct 1655.
    p 212
    Bought 100 acres from Ben Powell. 19 Nov 1652. p 216
Dudley, Edwd. With Wm Downman and Ben Powell is assigned 300 acres
    on Grynes Creek by Jno Sharpe. 6 Feb 1651/2. p 119
    To pay levy on 1 tytheable to Mr Tho Brice. 6 Feb 1654/5. p 174
Dun', Arth: On his complaint the Court orders John Philips to "make
    a sirvey" of land sold him by Abra Moone. That Mr Bartram
    Hobart, Mr Willis, Tho Kid and Evan Davies be present and re-
    port to this Court. 6 June 1655. p 196
    Non-suit to him in case of Abra Moone who failed to appear.
    6 June 1655. p 198
Dune, Arther. Wit deed Keds to Pattison and Bridges. 16 April 1655.
    p 219
Dunstan, Wm. Headright of Mr Rd Perrott. 6 Oct 1653. p 77

Eaton, George. deceased. His estate owes Mr David Fox 5 "Anchors of
    dram". Order for paymt. 10 Jan 1652/3. p 28
    His admr Jno Hunt. See entry Jno Sharpe. 6 Apl 1653. p 44
    His land adj patent of Row Lawson on Rappa. 6 June 1655. p 205

Eaton, Jno. deceased, merchant. P of A to Cuth: Potter from Jno
    Custise of Northampton Co, merchant, to collect a/cs from his
    admrs. 26 July 1653. p 88
    Whereas Cuth: Potter atty of Jno Custice hath impleaded John
    Sharpe attorney of Jno Hunt and Tho: Harwood the admrs of John
    Eaton deceased for a debt of 300 lb tobo, judgmt is issued agst
    Eaton's estate. 8 Dec 1653. p 97
Eaton, Kath: Headright of Nich Feyman (or Fepman) 6th Feb 1653/4.
    p 139
Ebbesonn, Anne. Wit mortgage Tho Carter to Jno Carter. 18 Sept 1655.
    p 228
Edgcombe, Jno. Sues Antho Jackman for land sold to him. 6 Oct 1652.
    p 15
    Buys 550 acres in Rappa on N side abt 37 miles up, from Antho
    Jackman. 29 Dec 1652. p 19
    Certificate for his own transportation into this Country. 6th
    April 1653. p 43
    To pay levy on 1 tytheable to Mr Toby Smith. 24 Oct 1653. p 92
    To pay levy on 2 tytheables to Mr Toby Smith. 6 Febry 1654/5.
    p 174
    His a/c incl in settlemt of Lawson estate. 20 Jan 1655/6. p 192
    Order that Jno Gregory and Jno Sherlock view the houseing built
    by him for Capt More Fantleroy and report. 6 June 1655. p 199
    Judgement agst him for debt of 1193 lb tobo with interest for
    2 yrs to Capt More Fantleroy. 6 June 1655. p 199
    Arrested for spreading scandle agst Capt Fantleroy and his wife.
    That the words were "darkely delivered". He is ordered to ask
    Capt Fantleroy's pardon at this Court and at the next Court to
    stand "with his Crime in Capitall letters printed on his hatt".
    6 June 1655. p 199
    To pay levy on 5 tytheables to Mr Griffin. 7 Dec 1655. p 236
    He and Sara his wife humbly confess and beg pardon publicly
    for having falsely defamed and scandalized Capt Moore Fantleroy,
    his wife and children. A long entry. Signed John Edgecombe.
    Sara x Edgecombe. Wit: James Bagnall. Richd Raddocke. 15 Sept
    1655. p 243
Edmonds, Elias, Had Wm Thatcher arrested who did not appear. Judgmt
    agst Wm Clapham Sr, Thatcher's security. 6 Apl 1653. p 43
    Order that he be pd 1000 lb tobo by Wm Thatcher for killing his
    hogs. 8 Aug 1653. p 63
    Several differences betw him and Robt Perfect to next Court. 6
    Oct 1653. p 77
    This entry as 'Mr Edmonds'. To pay levy on 4 tytheables to Mr
    Row Lawson. 24 Oct 1653. p 90
    Dif with Epe Bonney to next Court. 9 Dec 1653. p 99
    Ordered to pay debt 300 lb tobo to Ebey Bonney. To be pd by
    Edwd Grimes who owes this amt to Edmonds. 6 Feb 1653/4. p 137
    Deceased. See entry Edwin Conway regarding his estate. 6 April
    1654. p 140

Edmonds, Elias. Deceased. Accounts to be pd from estate by John
Meredith and Walter Heard. The est to be appraised by Mr
Clapham senior, Mr Edwin Conaway and Mr Jno Edwards. Levies
and fees to be pd first. 6 June 1654. p 144
His estate ordered to pay Wm Clapham Sr 558 lb tobo. 6 June
1654. p 145
Judgt agst Jno Meredith the admr to Jno Edwards, chirurgeon,
for "Phisick administered" to him and his wife. 6 June 1654.
p 145
His land on N side of E branch of Corotomen River, adj Dr Jno
Edwards. 19 Oct 1653. p 149
Order that Jno Meredith and Walter Herd his admrs pay Marg:
Grimes, widow, for 3 mos dyet for a servant. 7 Aug 1654. p 151
His admr, Walter Hord (John Meredith joint admr) to be reliev-
ed. 6 June 1655, p 199
Use of his cattle to Jno Meredith for bringing up the children.
Quitus est on his estate to Meredith. 25 Oct 1655. p 211
Edmonds, Frances. Wife and exbrx of Elias Edmonds dec'd. She died
intestate and "whereas John Meridith her sonne in law and
Walter Herd her own sonne" petition for letters of admr. This
granted. Wm Clapham Junr and Jno Sharpe securities. 7 March
1653/4. p 142
Edwards, John. Headright of Oliver Segar. 6 Aug 1653. p 62
Edwards, Mr. To pay levy on 4 tytheables to Mr Tho Brice. 24th Oct
1653. p 91
Edwards, Jno. To appraise est of Elias Edmonds decd. 6 June 1654.
p 144
Edwards, Jno. Chirurgeon. Ordered to refund 1/2 pmt of 470 lb tobo
made by Walter Flemingo for the cure of his leg in which he
failed. 6 June 1654. p 144
Judgt to him agst est of Elyas Edmonds for "phisick administer-
ed" to him and his wife. 6 June 1654. p 145
Judgt agst him to Jno Meridith admr of est of Elias Edmonds for
1835 lb tobo. 6 June 1654. p 145
Buys 300 acres from Tho Burroughs 16 June 1653. Sells it to
Walter Dickeson prior to 1655. Date not shown. p 148
Has Grant, 19 Oct 1653, 350 acres on N side of E branch of
Corotomen River, adjs land of Elyas Edmonds, etc. Jno Edwards
sells this land to Tho Ball of Northampton Co., Va., mariner.
"this last of Deber Ano Domy 1653". Wit: Jas Butt. Anto:
Hogkins. p 149
Ordered to return a hhd tobo pd by Abra Moone for setting a
dislocated shoulder and no cure effected. 6 Feb 1654/5. p 171
Edwards, Mr. To pay levy on 4 tytheables to Mr Tho Brice. 6th Feb
1654/5. p 174
Edwards, Jno. Wit deed Borough to Hopkins. 5 Feb 1654/5. p 180
Wit deed Fox to Bourough. 5 Feb 1654/5. p 180
Wit Roughton to Brathatt. 27 Sept 1655. p 216

Eeevns, Tho. Binds himself to deliver to Edw Lylly "a drauft of a
parcell of Land" which he took up in Rappa River abt 12 miles
up. Says he has Lillys bills for 1000 lb tobo in paymt. Wit.Tho
Mannyng. 7 March 1652/3. p 36
Elliott, Lt Col An: Sues Lambert Lamberson for 4500 lb tobo as
attorney of Tho Purifye. 6 Feb 1653/4. p 138
Elliott, Arth: Headright of Clemt: Thrush. 6 Oct 1652. p 15
Ellis, Alice. Headright of Edwin Conway. 6 Oct 1652. p 15
Elsmore, Danl. Headright of Jno Weir. 6 Oct 1654. p 162
Eltonhead, Mr Wm. See entry Sir Hen Chicheley. 18 Apl 1654. p 129
Eltonhead family detail. See entry Edwin Conway. 15 May 1653. p 69
Emere, Tho. Headright of Capt More Fantleroy. 10 Jan 1652/3. p 27
Emerson, Nycho: Headright of Capt More Fantleroy. 10 Jan 1652/3.p.27
Emerson, Wm. Headright of Jo Paine. 6 Aug 1655. p 209
English, Kath: Headright of Mr Row Lawson. 6 Feb 1654/5. p 172
Evans see Eeevns.
Eveens, Thos. Patented 250 acres abt 20 miles up on North side of
Rappahannock. 30 August 1643. Recorded 12 Jan 1652/3. p 37
Eward, Seath. Headright of Mr Toby Smith. 7 Aug 1654. p 151
Eyres, Joan. Headright of Jo: Eyers. 6 Aug 1655. p 208
Eyers, Jo: Certificate for land for importing 4 persons: Jno Taylor,
Joan Eyres, Elinor Gill, Hen: Peeters. 6 Aug 1655. p 208
To pay levy on 2 tytheables to Jno Paine. 7 Dec 1655. p 239

Falldo, Mrs. See entry Tho Whettell. 11 May 1651. p 6
Fauntleroy, Captain Moore. Appears almost invariably in these
records as Capt More Fantleroy.
Fantleroy, Capt More. Certificate for 200 acres for importing 4
persons: 'Moroway a hylander', Eliza Whitehead, An: Chester,
and - (illegible). 1 July 1652. p 1
Having entered 3 actions agst the body of Nathaniell Baytson
all returned 'non est inventus', etc. 6 Aug 1652. p 3
Deed showing him as of Lancaster Co. Sells Tho Roots 300 acres
on E side of Farnham Creek, adj Leroy Griffin, Thomas Griffin.
Wit: Toby Smith, Howell Powell. 8 July 1652. p 7
Grant of 200 acres in Rappa River abt 44 miles on S side. 18th
April 1651. This land assigned to "my brother in law Toby Smith
gent" and heirs begotten of Phebe his wife. 24 Oct 1651. p 12
Grant of 350 acres in Rappa River on S side adj and above 200
acres formerly taken up by him. 22 May 1650. This land assigned
to "my brother in law Toby Smith gent" and his heirs begotten
of Phebe his wife. 24 Oct 1651. p 13
Sues Ralph Paine but fails to appear. Case dismissed. 6th Oct
1652. p 17
His land adjs Jackman Creek, land granted to Antho Jackman, etc.
29 Dec 1652. p 19
Several actions agst Danl Baytson who is ordered to pay 5515
lb tobo and costs of suits. 10 Jan 1652/3. p 26

Fantleroy, Capt More. Certificate for importing 20 persons into this
    Country. (names distributed through this volume. Not listed
    here to save space). 10 Jan 1652/3. p 27
    Judgt to him agst Nathl Baytson for 96 arms length of Roanoke,
    5515 lb tobo, a gun sold by him to the Indians, etc. 10th Jan
    1652/3. p 28
    Pd 2500 lb tobo from County levy. Does not state what for but
    perhaps for burgess charge. 10 Jan 1652/3. p 29
    Deed of Gift. 22 Sept 1653. Gives LeRoy Griffin the son of Thos
    Griffin of Lancaster Co, 300 acres on Farnham Creek on the
    river side. If he die before 21 the land to his father. Wit:
    Alex Cooke Clr. Benjamin Helliard. p 74
    Deed. 22 Sept 1653. Sells Mr Thomas Griffin 620 acres adj land
    belonging to LeRoy Griffin son of Tho Griffin. The land S.W. on
    the river, etc. Wit: Alex Cooke Clk. Benjamin Heliard. p 75
    Order that he report on boundries betw Tho Paine and Hen Dedman.
    6 Oct 1653. p 78
    Judgt agst Mr David Fox for 3 bbl corn. 24 Oct 1653. p 89
    In County expense in levy. Mr Toby Smith "To pay Ca Fantleroy
    to Patrick for Attendance on the Burgesses" 150 lb tobo. 24th
    Oct 1653. p 92
    To pay levy on 4 tytheables to Mr Toby Smith. 24 Oct 1653. p 92
    In County expense in levy "for Expences and provision going to
    Ja Cittye Burges 0620 lb tobo". 24 Oct 1653. p 95
    Dif betw him and Tho Paine to next Court. 9 Dec 1653. p 100
    Ordered to pay debt of 6 bbl corn to Mr Tho Paine. 9 Dec 1653.
    p 100
    To be pd for a sloop lost by Mychaell Winsmore. 9 Dec 1653.
    p 101
    A power of atty from Tho Paine to Mr Raleigh Travers to sue
    him. 6 Dec 1653. p 103
    Pays Wm Neesam and Jno Meriman 3500 lb tobo due from estate of
    Epa Lawson dec'd. 6 June 1654. p 145
    See entry Edw Boswell. 6 June 1654. p 146
    His suit agst Mr Tho Griffin dismissed. 6 Feb 1654/5. p 174
    To pay levy on 7 tytheables to Mr Toby Smith. 6 Feb 1654/5.
    p 174
    His a/c incl in settlemt of Lawson estate. 20 Jan 1655/6. p 192
    Judgmt 446 lb tobo agst estate of Thos Walker in his hands to
    Mr Tho Griffin. 6 June 1655. p 197
    Scandal spread about him, his wife and children by Jno Edgcomb
    who is severely punished for it. See entry in his name. 6 June
    1655. p 199
    Judgt to him agst Jno Edgcomb for debt of 1193 lb tobo with
    interest for 2 yrs. 6 June 1655. Edgcomb
    A house built for him by Jno/Sherlock to be viewed and reported
    on by Jno Gregory and Jno Sherlock. 6 June 1655. p 199
    To pay levy on 5 tytheables to Mr Griffin. 7 Dec 1655

Fantleroy, Capt Moore. Apologised to by John and Sara Edgecombe. See
     entry their names. 15 Sept 1655. p 243
Fauntleroy family detail. See entry Toby Smith. 29 Sept 1647. p 81-2
Fargen, Cornelia. Headright of Capt Henry Fleet. 6 June 1655. p 198
Fellett, Mr. To pay levy on 6 tytheables to Mr Felson. 7 Dec 1655.
     p 238
Felps, Da: Certificate for the transportation of himself twice, Tho
     Humphreys, Eliz Colloins (this name subject to correction), Tho
     Smythson, Mr Jno Cox twice and Tho Thorpe. 6 Feb 1653/4. p 139
Felson, Mr. The County is indebted to him 300 lb tobo for provisions
     "in the march". 7 Dec 1655. p 233
     To receive levy for 27 tytheables from 9 persons incl 4 for
     himself. 7 Dec 1655. p 238
Fenwick. See entry Edwin Conway who refers to "my sister Fenwick".
     15 May 1653. p 69
Ferey, Ben. Headright of Mr Toby Smith. 6 Oct 1652. p 16
Ferman, Nich. Security for Jno Pedro in debt of 400 lb tobo. 8 Dec
     1653. p 96
     To "vew" Mr Rawleigh Travers' tobacco house and report. 6 Feb
     1654/5. p 172
     Wit deed Fox to Bourough. 5 Feb 1654/5. p 180
Ferman possibly identical with Feyman. See below.
Ferry. To transport passengers from Grimes Cove or Island Point. Col
     Clayborne to agree for Northumberland Co. The Commissioners for
     Gloster and York to be notified, etc. 9 Dec 1653. p 101
Feyman, Nick. To view work done by Jno Pedro for Mr Row Burnham and
     report. 6 Oct 1653. p 77
     Certificate for transportation of 3 persons. Jane Nickson, Kath
     Eaton, Jno Burne. 6 Feb 1653/4. p 139
Firment, Samuel. His a/c incl in settlemt of Lawson estate. 20 Jan
     1655/6. p 192
Fisher, Wm. Headright of Jas Bonner. 25 Oct 1655. p 210
Fleet, Captain Henry.
     Judgt confessed to him 1120 lb tobo by Mr Rich: Loes. 6th Oct.
     1652. p 16
     He and Mr Wm Underwood pd 3305 lb tobo from the County levy.
     Does not state what for. 10 Jan 1652/3. p 29
     See entry 'Muster'. 8 Aug 1653. p 65
     One of 21 of his headrights was Jno Brint. 24 Oct 1653. p 89
     Justice. 24 Oct 1653. p 89
     To pay levy on 12 tytheables to Mr Row Lawson. 24 Oct 1653.
     p 90
     In County levy 300 lb tobo to be pd "To Ca: Fleet for Jesper"
     24)ct 1653. p 90
     Judgt confessed to him for 777 lb tobo by Margaret Grimes,
     relict and extrx of Edw Grimes dec'd. 9 Dec 1653. p 98
     Justice. 9 Dec 1653. p 98
     Judgt confessed to him by Wm Newsam exor of Robt Mascall decd
     for 420 lb tobo. 9 Dec 1653. p 100

Fleet, Captain Henry.
      Justice. 16 May 1654. p 131
      Patent. 200 acres in Lancaster Co., in Fleets Bay, S. upon
      Hadaways Creek and upon the bay, N. into the woods, W. on a
      branch of Hadaways Creek "including the three Indyan Cabins".
      1 Aug 1652. p 132.   Fleet assigns the foregoing to John
      Sharpe. Wit: Toby Smith. Wm Ball. No date. Recognit 8 Dec.
      Recorded 10 die etc 1653. p 132
      Justice. 6 June 1654. p 144
      Justice. 7 Augt 1654. p 151
      Justice. 6 Feb. 1654/5. p 171
      Judgt to him, as assignee of Wm Booth, agst estate of Richd:
      Lake dec'd for 1302 lb tobo to be pd by Geo Kibble admr. 6th
      Feb 1654/5. p 173
      To collect levy on 26 tytheables incl 11 tytheables of his own
      family. 6 Feb 1654/5. p 174
      Regarding patent 200 acres of 1 Aug 1652 (see above). John
      Sharpe now assigns his interest in the land to Hugh Brent. Wit:
      Tho Madestard. Dower rights relinq by Elenor Sharp wife of Jno
      Sharp. Wit: John x Robinson. 11 Dec 1654. p 187
      Justice. 6 June 1655. p 196
      Certificate for importing 9 persons. 6 June 1655. p 198
      Order that he "shall summond sume of the great men of Wickocomi-
      i-koe and demand satisfacon for trespasses done by them to Tho
      Bourne and other men on the S side of the river". 6 June 1655.
      p 198
      Justice. 25 Oct 1655. p 210
      To be pd debt of 550 lb tobo by Jno Robinson. 25 Oct 1655.p 212
      Payments to be made him by -illegible- of 1877 lb tobo. 25 Oct
      1655. p 212
      Buys 700 acres from Wm Clapham formerly bought by Clapham from
      Mr Rd Bennett Esq. See entry Clapham for detail. 30 June 1655.
      p 229
      Justice. 7 Dec 1655. p 231
      To receive levy on 43 tytheables from:

Capt Fleet	16
Teage Floyne	1
Toby Horton	6
Ebby Bonnison	5
Mr Row Lawson	4
Will'm Harper	2
Jo Brathat	1
Sam Sloper	1
Mr Clappam	4
Capt Fleets upper plantacon	3

                     7 Dec 1655. p.235.
      To pay himself 349 lb tobo from County levy "To himself for
      caske upon the Burgesses bill to Jo: Baldwyn". 7 Dec 1655.
      p 235
      Justice. 6 Jan 1655/6. p 244.

Fleets Bay. 1 Aug 1652. p 132

Fleminge, Mr. To pay levy on 4 tytheables to Mr Jno Paine. 7th Dec
    1655. p 239

Flaminge, Alex. Wit mortgage Nicholls to Linell. 30 Nov 1653. p 105

Fleming, Elex. Assigned land by Wm Moseley. 6 Aug 1655. p 214

Fleminge, Walter. Petitions agst Jno Edwards chirurgeon who he paid
    470 lb tobo to cure his sore leg, which he did not do. Edwards
    ordered to repay half. 6 June 1654. p 144
      Is sued by Tobyas Horton for failing to cure a sore leg. See
      entry his name. 6 Feb 1654/5. p 171

Flid, Teague. Certificate for land for importing himself and Eliz
    his wife. 6 Oct 1652. p 15

Flinte, Rd. Sues Andrew Boyer and his wife. Is non-suited. 6 April
    1653. p 43

Flynt, Richd. with Wm Wraughton patents 200 acres on W side Coroto-
    men 29 Nov 1652. Assigns his interest to Wraughton 23rd Nov.
    1653. p 116

Flint, Richd. 400 acres formerly surveyed for him and Wm Raughton,
    sold by Raughton to Brathat. 27 Sept 1655. p 216

Flood, Joane and John. Headrights of Clemt Thrush. 6 Oct 1652. p 15

Flower, Nicho: Wit deed Harwood to Sharpe. 26 June 1651. p 119

Floyne, Teague. Possibly appears as Teague Flid. See above.

Floyne, Teague. To be pd 15 lb tobo having been subpoenaed by John
    Hunt. 6 Oct 1652. p 17

Floyne, Teague. Constable for this year. 6 Apl 1653. p 44

Floyne, Teague. Has impleaded Thomas Hardinge for assault and
    battery. It appears "Many abusive ill languages were rendered
    by both of them to each other". Both to put in security for
    good behavior. Hardinge to pay Floyne 1500 lb tobo for injury.
    This is a quaint and interesting entry. 6 Aug 1653. p 61

Floyne, Teage. Judgt agst him 400 lb tobo to Lambert Lamberson for
    his cure for being hurt. 6 August 1653. p 61

Floyne, Teage. Was extremely injured by Tho Hardinge "with stamping
    on his breast with his foot". Record of 6 Aug 1653. p 61

Floyne, Teage. (entered merely as 'Teage') To pay levy on 2 tythe-
    ables to Mr Da: Fox. 24 Oct 1653. p 91

Floyne, Teage. Committed for good behavior last August to be re-
    leased. 9 Dec 1653. p 101.   (The Constable !!)

Floyne, Teage. To pay levy on 3 tytheables to Capt Hen Fleet. 6 Feb
    1654/5. p 174. (Note: The old Captain was evidently not afraid
    to collect taxes from him. I rather think I would have been.BF)

Fookes, Jno. Sells 100 acres of land for the County's use. 25 Oct
    1655. p 210

Foote, Wm. deceased. Admr to Wm Clapham for a debt of 700 lb tobo.
    est to be appraised by Wm Neesham and Edw Tennies. 10 Jan
    1652/3. p 23

Forrett, Hen: See entry Rd. Lake. 7 Oct 1653. p 109

Foster, Ed. Headright of Mr Ja Bagnell. 6 Aug 1655. p 208

Foster, Hen: Headright of Mr Toby Smith. 6 Oct 1652. p 16

Fox, Mr David.
  Justice. 1 July 1652. p 1
  Complains that Thomas Brooks has made foul aspersions agst his
  wife, Mrs Mary Fox. Brooks ordered to acknowledge his offense
  in Court and at the "next meeting when there shall be a sermon"
  6 August 1652. p 2
  Justice. 6 Aug 1652. p 2
  Buys 1400 acres from Tho Burbage. 5 June 1652. p 14
  Certificate for importing 6 persons. 6 Oct 1652. p 15
  Justice. 6 Oct 1652. p 15
  Judgt confessed to him 3400 lb tobo by Lambert Lamberson. 10th
  Jan 1652/3. p 23
  The estate of Geo Eaton owes him 5 "anchors of dram". Order for
  paymt. 10 Jan 1652/3. p 28
  Pd 60 lb tobo from County levy for a book. 10 Jan 1652/3. p 29
  Letter from his house written by Rev Alex Cooke. See entry his
  name. 26 Sept 1652. pp 41-2
  Justice. 6 Apl 1653. p 43
  To be pd a "Matche coate" by Andrew Boyer for an Indian that
  had been shot by Boyer. 6 Apl 1653. p 43
  Statement sworn before him as Justice. 24 Feb 1652/3. p 45
  Justice. 6 Aug 1653. p 61
  Challenged to dual by Capt Tho Hackett. See entry his name. 8th
  Aug 1653. p 63
  The Court continued at his house. 8 Aug 1653. p 63
  See entry 'Muster'. 8 Aug 1653. p 65
  Judgt confessed to him 2000 lb tobo by Geo Gilling. 6 Oct 1653.
  p 78
  Will give evidence in action of debt Danl Howes agst Wm White.
  26 May 1653. p 87
  Justice. 24 Oct 1653. p 89
  Judgt agst him for 3 bbl corn to Capt Fantleroy. 24 Oct 1653.
  p 89
  To collect levy for 36 tytheables incl 10 tytheables of his own
  family. 24 Oct 1653. p 91
  To be pd from County levy 150 lb tobo for a wolf's head. 24th
  Oct 1653. p 95
  Justice. 8 Dec 1653. p 96
  See entry Cuth: Potter. 30 Nov 1653. p 117
  Wit will of Edw Grime. 1 Aug 1653. p 124
  Justice. 6 June 1654. p 144
  His land adjs a patent of Hen Hackery. 1 Sept 1651. p 148
  A Court at his house 7 Aug 1654. p 151
  Attaches estate of Capt Tho Hacket for 795 lb tobo. 7 Aug 1654.
  p 153
  Justice. 6 Oct 1654. p 163
  Justice. 6 Feb 1654/5. p 171
  Judgt to him agst Tho Griffin for debt of 780 lb tobo. 6 Feb
  1654/5. p 171

Fox, Mr. David.
  His name, with Mr Toby Smith and Mr Ja: Bagnall, presented to
  the Governor for election of sheriff. 6 Feb 1654/5. p 172
  To collect levy on 49 tytheables incl 16 tytheables of his own
  family. 6 Feb 1654/5. p 174
  Grant to David Fox, gent, 1 Nov 1653. 300 acres known as Narow
  Neck, on W side Corotomen River, adj land of Wm Wraughton and
  Rich Flinte. On 3 March 1653/4 he sells it to Tho Bourough.
  Wit: Nicho Ferman. Jno Edwards. p 180
  His son-in-law, Arth: Clearke, desires Mr Tho Griffin be his
  guardian instead of Mr Fox. See entry Clearke. 6 June 1655.
  p 200
  To deliver to Arther Clarke all cattle belonging to him. 25th
  Oct 1655. p 211
  To receive levy on 52 tytheables from 10 persons, including 14
  tytheables for himself. 7 Dec 1655. p 238
Fox family memo: At the risk of being prolix the following is included. In the Northumberland County records, Vol.15 pages 144-
  145, there is an item mutilated but interesting. Power of Atty
  dated London, 22 Sept 1664. Geo Hardinge, citizen and grocer
  of London and Mary Hardinge his wife dau of Tho Orley of London
  and Anne his wife dec'd, and sister of -torn away- -Orley late
  of Cherry Poynt in Potomack decd, to -torn away- - to demand
  from Rebecca Orley late wife and extrx of the will of the said
  Tho Orley of Cherry Pt decd and from Wm Jollins, her now
  husband, planter, money, etc. Then this entry follows which is
  not clear. However it appears that someone was told to "go
  search the Register Church Booke of the Parish churge of St.
  Mary White Chappell did find that the above declared Mary Orley
  daughter of Tho and Anne Orley was Baptized on the 25th of
  Aprill 1622". Dated London 29 Sept 1664. This entry confused
  me, there being St. Mary's White Chapel in Lancaster Co., Va.
  I sent a copy of the entries to Dr. Brydon. This was included
  in his reply "The St. Mary's Whitechapel of 1622 was St. Mary's
  Church in White Chapel District of London. St. Mary's in Lanc.
  was named for St. Mary's Wopl of London, thro influences of the
  Fox family I think". Dr. Brydon told me afterwards that David
  Fox was of this parish in London.   B.F.
Foxcroft, Daniell. 600 lb tobo to be allowed to Marga Grimes for a
  steer she sold him. 6 Oct 1654. p 164
Foxell, Sarah. Headright of Danl Welch. 6 Aug 1653. p 62
Franklin, Rich: Headright of D. Theriott. 6 Oct 1652. p 16
Fry, Mary. Headright of Capt Hen: Fleet. 24 Oct 1653. p 89
Fulgam, Antho. Wit Powell, Paine, Sneade transaction. 5 Dec 1652.
  p 48

Galsworthy see Garlesworthy.
Garber, Wm. Wit deed Lewis to Willis and Watkins. 4 Jan 1653/4.p.155
Garlesworthy, Wm. Headright of Robt Tomlyn. 6 Oct 1653. p 78
Gates, Jas. To be pd debt of 600 lb tobo by Jno Robinson for a cow.
  25 Oct 1655. p 212

Geery, Wm and Oliver. Wit: P of A Lea to Sheares (London). 20 Sept 1649. p 5

Gemies (?) Edw. pd 100 lb tobo from County levy for his boat. 10th Jan 1652/3. p 29

George, Mr. His land adj Capt Tho Hackett, Jno Nicholls on E side Corotomen River. 24 Jan 1653/4. p 165

George, Jon. Headright of Capt More Fantleroy. 10 Jan 1652/3. p 27

George, Nichloas

"Loveinge Friende John Nicklis my kind love Remembered unto your self and your wife and Children and all the rest of our ould Naighbours I Received your Letter and wonder that you should tax me with Fooling you which allways desired to be your friend neither will I any way in the world wronge you neither would I have you doubt my word in the least manner concerning any agreement made betwixt us: for my desire is to doe you any good I can which I am certayne I can doe little heare thru share for my wift shee is very onwilling to come by Reason of the dangers shee conceavs are by watter notwithstanding as farr as lay in mee I cleared all doubts to hir concerning that and to give you further sattisfaction i provided that I have the upper parte of the Land you live upon you may dispose of the lower part to Naighbours your self as you shall finde convenant not else but our Respects to you all wee shall Remaine your loveing Friend Nickloas George. Your cosen Taverner and his wife desire to be Remembered to you you shall heare further by the next Returne if convonancie will permite this 30th of October 1652"

Recorded 8 Jan 1652. (1652/3)
Teste John Phillips.   page 36

George, Nicholas. Agreemt with John Nicholls to divide 700 acres equally. Wit: Tho Taberery. 13 June 1653. p 115. (Note: The name of the witness is as shown here. It is not Tho Zakerery. Possibly it is the best Mr Phillips could make of Cousin Taverner's signature. B.F.)

George, Nichollas. His land on E side of N W branch of Corotomen River. See entry Jno Nicholls. 22 Dec 1652. p 114

Geyar, Elliner. To pay levy on 1 tytheable to Abra Weekes. 7th Dec. 1655. p 237

Gill, Elinor. Headright of Jo Eyers. 6 Aug 1655. p 208

Gill, Jno. Headright of Capt More Fantleroy. 10 Jan 1652/3. p 27

Gillett, Jno. Inventory of goods in his hands of Mr Robt Vivran decd. 12 Jan 1652/3. p 38

Constable for this year. 6 Apl 1653. p 44

Dif betw him and Robt Tomlyn to next Court. 6 Oct 1653. p 77

To pay levy on 4 tytheables to Mr Andrew Gilson. 24 Oct 1653. p 94

Gillett, John. This entry as 'Jno Gellet'. To pay 700 lb tobo to
   estate of Robt Vivian dec'd for land "to be found out and surveyed". 9 Dec 1653. p 98. (This certainly was a pig in the
   bag. I wonder what he got. B.F.)
   Dif betw him and Robt Tomlyn to next Court. 9 Dec 1653. p 101
   Nonsuit in his action agst Rob: Tomblin for non appearance at
   two Courts. 6 Apl 1654. p 141
   Certificate for transportation of 8 persons. 6 Oct 1654. p 162
   Patent. 4 Feb 1653/4. 200 acres on S side Rappa, on SW side of
   Gilsons Creek, adj land of Mr Bartho: Hogskins, etc. Jno Gillet
   assigns this land to Jno Greene. Wit: Jno Weir. Robt Tomlines.
   6 Oct 1654. p 167
   To pay levy on 4 tytheables to Mr And Gilson. 6 Feb 1654/5. 2
   p 174
Gilling, Geo: Confesses judgt to Mr David Fox for 2000 lb tobo. 6th
   Oct 1653. p 78
   To be pd 455 lb tobo from levy by Mr Rd Perrott for attendance
   on the burgesses. 24 Oct 1653. p 93
Gilson, Mr Andrew.
   Justice. 6 Oct 1652. p 15
   Justice. 10 Jan 1652/3. p 23
   Appraises goods of Robt Vivran decd. 12 Jan 1652/3. p 38
   See entry 'Muster'. 8 Aug 1653. p 65
   Justice. 6 Oct 1653. p 77
   To collect levy from 7 persons on 29 tytheables including 4
   tytheables of his own family. 24 Oct 1653. p 94
   Justice. 9 Dec 1653. p 98
   Justice. 6 Apl 1654. p 140
   Certificate for importing 5 persons. 6 Oct 1654. p 162
   Justice 6 Oct 1654. p 162
   Wit deed Taylor to Tomlyn. 6 Oct 1654. p 166
   An appeal to General Court by Mr Robt Tomlin in land dif. with
   him. 6 Feb 1654/5. p 171
   To collect levy on 33 tytheables incl 4 tytheables of his own.
   6 Feb 1654/5. p 174
   To admr oath to appraisers of est of Paul Brewer. 6 June 1655.
   p 201.
   Justice. 6 Aug 1655. p 207
Gilson, Antho. To appraise est of Robt Vivian decd. 6 Oct 1652. p 16
Gilson, George. Justice. 1 July 1652. p 1
Gilson, Mr. His creek and plantation. See entry Markets. 6 June 1655.
   p 201
Girton, Jno. Headright of Hugh Brent. 6 Feb 1654/5. p 171
Glascooke, Mr. To pay levy on 3 tytheables to Mr Griffin. 7th Dec
   1655. p 236
Godwin, Tho. His land adj grant to Jas Bonner on S side Rappa. 15th
   Sept 1651. p 147
Godwin, Tho. Patent to him and Richd Axome. 22 May 1650. 1000 acres
   in Rappa River adj Brecknock Bay, the land of Jno Lanman, etc.
   p 168

Godwin, Thos. Wit deed James to Best and Aschley. Is entered as 28
    Aug 1651 but is actually 1654. pp 184-5
Goldsmith, Mrs. Her land on E side N W branch Corotomen. See entry
    Jno Nicholls. 22 Dec 1652. p 114
Goldsmith, Geo. Wit deed Clapham Jr to Steephenson. 12 July 1654.
    p 188
Gooch, Mary. Bequest from Edw Grime. 1 Aug 1653. p 124
Gooch, Saml. Wit: Lylly to Keegam and Pine. 7 Sept 1652. p 40
    Signs statement regarding wages for a servant to be pd Mr Rd.
    Parett. 24 Feb 1652/3. p 45
Gooch, Samuell of Lancaster Co. Pre-nuptial agreemt. Marriage in-
    tended with Mary dau of Tho Adawoll dec'd regarding certain
    cattle left her by her father. Refers to Edw Grimes and Marg:
    (Margaret) his wife late relict of said Attawell, etc. 16th
    March 1652. p 123
Goodayell, Edw. Headright of Capt More Fantleroy. 10 Jan 1652/3.p 27
Goodale, Geo. Headright of Mr Row Lawson. 6 Feb 1654/5. p 172
Gookin, Capt Danl. Patented 1400 acres 4 Nov 1642 and assigned it
    to Tho Burbage who sold it to David Fox on 5 June 1652. p 14
Gossage, Robt. To pay levy to V. Stanford. 7 Dec 1655. p 235
Gower, Fra: Certificate for transportation of 4 persons. 24th Oct
    1653. p 89
    To pay levy on 3 tytheables to Mr Ja Williamson. 6 Feb 1654/5.
    p 174
    To appraise estate of Tho Meads dec'd. 6 June 1655. p 197
    To pay levy on 2 tytheables to Mr Wm Underwood. 7 Dec 1655.
    p 234
Gramer, Tho. Headright of Jno Gillet. 6 Oct 1654. p 162
Grasher a Negro. To whip delinquents but not to attend Court. 25th
    Oct 1655. p 213
Greene, Eliz: Has Grant of her part of Herd's patent. 7 Dec 1655.
    p 231
    Appears as Eliz Greene als Hutchins, and as wife of Wm Hutchins.
    See entry John Bond regarding her land. 4 Dec 1655. pp 241-2
Greene, Jno. Bought 200 acres on S W side of Gilsons Creek from Jno
    Gillet. 6 Oct 1654. p 167
    To be pd from County levy for "one wolfe kild". 6 Feb 1654/5.
    p 173
Greene, Sary. Headright of Mr Edmond Kemp. 25 Oct 1655. p 213
Greene, Tho. Headright of Capt More Fantleroy. 10 Jan 1652/3. p 27
Gregory, Jno. To pay levy on 1 tytheable to Mr Toby Smith. 24 Oct
    1653. p 92
    To pay levy on 3 tytheables to Mr Ja Bagnall. 6 Feb 1654/5.
    p 174
    To view house built by Jno Edgcomb for Capt Fantleroy and
    report to this Court. 6 June 1655. p 199
    Assigned all interest in a patent by Wm Johnson. 14 Aug 1654.
    p 218
    To pay levy on 3 tytheables to Mr Bagnall. Also to be pd 150
    lb tobo from the levy for a wolf's head. 7 Dec 1655. p 236

Griffin, Mr. To be pd 150 lb tobo from County levy for a wolf's
head. 24 Oct 1653. p 95
Griffen, Mr. To pay levy on 5 tytheables to Mr Toby Smith. 6th Feby
1654/5. p 174
Griffin, Mr. To receive levy on 25 tytheables from 6 persons incl
7 tytheables for himself. 7 Dec 1655. p 236
Griffin, Mr. To pay levy on 2 tytheables to Mr Bagnall. 7 Dec 1655.
p 236
Griffin, Leroy. His land on E side Farnham Creek adj Tho Griffin and
land sold by Fantleroy to Tho Roots. 8 July 1652. p 7
Has gift of land from More Fantleroy. See entry his name. 22nd
Sept 1653. p 74
Griffin, Thomas. Certificate for importing 4 persons. 10 Jan 1652/3.
p 24
Buys 620 acres from More Fantleroy. This land adj land belong-
ing to Le Roy Griffin son of Tho Griffin, S.W. on Rappa River
etc. 22 Sept 1653. p 75
Order that admrs of Epa Lawson decd pay him 3000 lb tobo as
assignee of Richd Lewis. 6 Oct 1653. p 79
To pay levy on 5 tytheables to Mr Toby Smith. 24 Oct 1653. p 92
Appears in entry as "Tho Griffin and Mynor". To pay levy on 2
tytheables to Mr Jas Bagnall. 24 Oct 1653. p 94
Sues Joane wife of Wm Thomas for slander. See entry her name.
9 Dec 1653. p 99
Obtains judgt agt cattle of Jno Pritchard for debt of 565 lb
tobo. 9 Dec 1653. p 99
Wit deed Boswell to Davies and Pedro. 16 May 1653. p 118
To pay Eliza Tomlyn certain goods. See entry her name. 6 Feb
1653/4. p 138
To appraise est of Tho Steephens decd. 7 Aug 1654. p 153
Judgt confessed to him by Enock Hauker 821 lb tobo. 6 Feb 1654/5
p 171
Judgt agst him to Mr Da: Fox for debt of 780 lb tobo. 6th Feb
1654/5. p 171
Has attachmt agst est of Tho Walker. 6 Feb 1654/5. p 173
Nonsuit to him on several suits of Capt More Fantleroy. 6 Feb
1654/5. p 174
Judgt to him agst est of Tho Walker in hands of Capt Fantleroy
for 446 lb tobo. 6 June 1655. p 197
Judgt to him as assignee of Wm Jon'son agst the est of Paul
Brewer for 700 lb tobo. 6 June 1655. p 197
Appointed guardian of Arth: Clearke (Clark). See entry his
name. 6 June 1655. p 200
To be pd 150 lb tobo from County levy by Mr Bagnall for a wolf's
head. 7 Dec 1655. p 236
Tho: Griffin and Tho Griffeth the same person ?. See witnesses
in entry Edw Boswell. 16 May 1653. 13 Nov 1653.
Griffeth, Mr. To be pd 150 lb tobo from County levy by Mr Toby
Smith for a wolf's head. 24 Oct 1653. p 92

Griffeth, Tho. Married the relict and extrx of Fra Marsh decd. 7th
   August 1654. p 151
      To be pd from County levy for 2 wolves' heads. 6 Feb 1654/5.
   p 173
      To pay levy on 1 tytheable to Mr Ja Bagnall. 6 Feb 1654/5.p 174
Griffeth, Tho of Rappahannock, Lancaster Co., planter. Mortgages
   crop and cattle to Mr Rich Loes of same Co., planter. Wit: Tho
   Madestard. John Millisent. 22 Nov 1654. p 182
Greefieth, Mr Tho. To pay fees Coupland vs Kemp. 25 Oct 1655. p 211
Greefeth, Tho. Wit assignmt of land Johnson to Gregory. 14 Aug 1654.
      p 218
Grigs, Mr. Sold a servant to Mr Rd Parett. 24 Feb 1652/3. See entry
   Parett's name. p 45
Grimes or Grymes. Also appears here as Grime.
Grimes, Edwd. He and Wm White "have Causlesly bene Arested" by Robt
   Mascall who is ordered to pay them damages. 8 Aug 1653. p 63
Grimes, Edw and Marg (Margaret) his wife, she late relict of Tho
   Adawell (Attawell), etc. See entry Saml Gooch. 16 Mar 1652/3.
      p 123
Grime, Edward. Will. Dated 1 Aug 1653. Prob 9 Dec 1653. To wife
   Margaret personal property if she remain single for life, other-
   wise to be div equally betw Wm Wraton, An White and Mary Gooch.
   To daughter in law Fra Attawell all land, 430 acres in Rappa
   river. She failing in heirs to Wm Wraton, he failing in heirs
   to An White and she failing to Mary Gooch. Wife exor. Super-
   visors Wm Newsam and Wm Wraton. Wit Davey Fox. Jno Phillips.
      p 124
Grimes, Edw. Appraised est of Hen Lee decd. 7 Mar 1652/3. p 126
   Owes Elias Edmonds 300 lb tobo. Ordered to pay Ebey Bonney.
   6 Feb 1653/4. p 137
   Wit: deed Powell to Downman. 19 Nov 1652. p 216
Grimes, Margaret. Relict and extrx of Edw Grimes confesses judgt to
   Capt Hen Fleet for 777 lb tobo. 9 Dec 1653. p 98
   As widow of Edw. See entry Cuth: Potter. 30 Nov 1653. p 117
   Her dau Fra: Attawell married Tho Roots chirurgeon. 14 Oct 1653.
      p 121
   Is assigned 300 acres for life by Tho Roots. 8 Dec 1653. p 122
   As widow, see entry Wm Clapham Jr. 6 June 1654. p 144
   Judgt agst her to Wm Clapham Jr for 130 lb tobo. 6 June 1654.
      p 146
   To be pd for 3 mos dyet for a servant of Elias Edmonds' estate.
   7 Aug 1654. p 151
   Two men employed to guard her house on death of an Indian. 6th
   Oct 1654. p 163
   To be allowed 600 lb tobo for a steer she sold Daniell Foxcroft.
   6 Oct 1654. p 164
   In entry as "Widow Grimes". To pay levy on 4 tytheables to Mr
   Tho Brice. 6 Feb 1654/5. p 174
   In entry as "the widow Grymes". A Court held at her house. 7th
   Dec 1655. p 231

Grimes Cove or Island Point. See entry Ferry. 9 Dec 1653. p 101
Grimes Cove. See entry Markets. 6 June 1655. p 201
Grymes Creek or Iland Neck Creek. See entry Tho Harwood. 14 Nov 1649.
   p 119
Grimes family (sic) To pay levy on 4 tytheables to Mr Tho Brice. 24
   Oct 1653. p 91
Grisley, Da: To pay the parish 1200 lb tobo for having a base born
   child by Marga Mealey. 6 Feb 1653/4. p 138
Gundry, Jo. (this entry not clear to me. B.F.). He requested Jo
   Phillips sheriff of Lancaster Co to present a/c of - tobo to
   the Commissioners of Lancaster Co to procure judgt agst John
   Merrid. Merrid is ordered to pay 237 lb tobo and costs. 25th
   Oct 1655. p 212
Gutteridge, Hen. Headright of Tho Griffin. 10 Jan 1652/3. p 24
Gwilliam, Geo. Wit Smith - Fantleroy of Nansemum. See entry Toby
   Smith. 29 Sept 1647. pp 81-2
Gyles, Mr Fra. Owes Epa Lawson L 22. 7. 0. 13 Apl 1651. p 9

Hackery, Henry. (Note: This name is not Zackery. It is not Thackery.
   The signature is plainly 'The marke of Hen: H Hackery'. B.F.)
   Patent. 1 Sept 1651. 300 acres on N side Corotomen river, adj
   S on land of David Fox, W on Moraticon path, etc. p 147. Hen:
   Hackery of the parish of York assigns this land to Thomas
   Burroughs. 9 Jan (year not shown). Wit: John Aduston. Thomas
   Ridly. p 148.   Thos Bourroughs assigns above land to John
   Edwards. Wit: Howell Powell. Tho: Hopkins. 16 June 1653. p 148.
   Jno Edwards 'surgeon' sells above to Walter Dickeson of
   Northampton Co, Va. for 3000 lb tobo. Wit: Jno Dollinge. Hen
   Vincent. 13 Aug 165-. p 148
Hacker, Henry. His land on W side Corotomen adjs Wm Wraughton. 29
   Nov 1652. p 116
Hacker, Rich. To pay levy on 1 tytheable to Mr Tho Bearn (Bourne).
   24 Oct 1653. p 92
Hackett, Mrs. Mary. See entry Tho. Hackett. 25 Oct 1655. p 226
Hackett, Captain Thomas. "Memorand that Tho: Hardinge hath made
   oath that he did transcribe a Chalenge (sent by Captt Hackett
   to Mr David Fox at this Court) at the request of the said
   Hackett in regard he wrote a fairer hand then the said Hackett".
   8 August 1653. p 63.
Richard Denham "sun in law to Cap'tt Thomas Hackett" delivered
   a challenge from his father-in-law (step father) to Mr David
   Fox during a sitting of Court. Asked if he knew what it was, he
   said he did. Whereupon Major Carter reproved him, etc. 8th
   Aug 1653. p 64
"The Chalenge ordered to be recorded
Mr Fox I wonder yu should see much degenerate from a gentleman
as to cast such an aspersion on me in open Court making
nothinge apeare but I know it to bee out of malice and an
evill disposicon which remaines in your heart therefore I

Hackett, Capt. Thomas (continued)
   desire yu if you have anything of a gentleman or of manhood in
   yu to meet me on towsday morning at the marked tree in the
   valley which parts your land and mine about eight of the Clock
   where I shall Expect your coming to give me satisfacon my
   weapon is Rapier the length I send you by this bearer not else
   at present but yours at the - apointed   Thomas Hackett
   Your second bringe alonge with yu if you please and I shall
   finde me of the like".   Recorded 10 August 1653. p 64
   Thos. Hackett ordered arrested and held by the sheriff until
   the next Quarter Court. He to answere before the Governor and
   Council.
Hackett, Capt. To pay levy on 3 tytheables to Mr Tho Brice. 24 Oct
   1653. p 91
Hackett, Capt Tho. Complains that Mary wife of John Robinson has
   abused his wife "callinge her begerly Jade and such like un-
   civill language". Mary Robinson ordered to acknowledge her
   sorrow for it before the minister and congregation. 8 Dec 1653.
   p 97
Hackett, Capt Tho. To appraise est of Wm Downman decd. 6 June 1654.
   p 145
Hacket, Capt Tho. His estate attached for 795 lb tobo at suit of Mr
   David Fox. 7 Aug 1654. p 153
Hackett, Capt Tho. Patent. 29 Nov 1652. 400 acres on E side Corotomen
   river, adj land of Mr Conaway, of Jno Nicolls, etc. Tho Hackett
   of Corotomen, planter, sells this land to John Nicholls for
   4000 lb tobo. Says the land adjs Mr Conaway and Mr George. Wit:
   Thomas Madestarde. Jno Millesent. 4 Jan 1653/4. p 165
Hacket, Capt. To pay levy on 2 tytheables to Mr Tho Brice. 6 Febry
   1654/5. p 174
Hackett, Tho. His land adj 400 acres sold by Tho and Howell Powell
   to Walter Herd. 19 Oct 1655. p 217
Hackett, Tho of Lancaster Co, gentleman. Leaveth to Mary his now
   wife, and to Richerde, Elle, William and Susanna Denhawes,
   children of the said Mary, 800 acres in Lancaster Co on upper
   N.W. side of Corotomen river, adj land of Mr John Seniour,
   E and SE on upper Corotomen River and SW on land of Wm Clapham
   now in possession of Tho Powell, N NW into the woods. Together
   with lands belonging to patent dated 9 June 1652. The forest
   lands as followeth: to Richards Denham, Little Neck containing
   200 acres adj the land of Mr John Seniour, Porriges Neck and
   land for John Sharpe: for John Sharpe the husband of Elinor
   Denham, 200 acres known as - (illegible but prob Porriges Neck)
   - and adj Dividing Creek: To Wm Denham a parcel next adj the
   land devised Jno Sharpe, the E side of Corotomen Path, Corotomen River being the residue of the 800 acres. Rights, however,
   to said Capt Tho Hackett's wife, Marie, during life. Wit: Tho
   Carter. Howell Powell. Signed Thomas Hackett. Dated 25th Oct
   1655. Recorded 25 Oct 1655. p 226
Hackett, Capt. To pay levy on 2 tytheables to Wm Neesham. 7 Dec 1655.
   p 237

Haddaway. This name is the old English Hathaway. I presume any
    remarks on this subject would be but an impertinence on my
    part. But still there may be a Roland for an Oliver. If so,
    here we are. B.F.
Haddaway, Row. To pay levy on 1 tytheable to Mr Tho Bearn. 24 Oct
    1653. p 92
    Wit deed Lake to Rigby. 5 Oct 1653. p 107
Hadaway, Rowland and his wife. To deliver up estate of Rd Lake on
    oath. 6 Oct 1654. p 162
Hadaway, Row. To pay levy on 2 tytheables to Mr Tho Bourne. 6 Feb
    1654/5. p 174
Hadway, Rowland. To pay levy on 2 tytheables to Mr Kemp. 7th Dec.
    1655. p 239
Hadaways Creek. At Fleets Bay. 1 Aug 1652. p 132. Also p 186
Hadwell see Attawell.
Haggett, Hum. Wit agreemt Littlepage with Cox. 16 Jan 1653/4. p 104
Hagett, Hump: Buys 400 acres from Nicho Meriwether 3 Oct 1654. Sells
    it to Cuth: Potter 30 Oct 1654. p 178
Hagett, Hum: Inquiry of the manner of his living with the wife of
    Tho Bacon who was hired to him to be made by Mr Edmond Kempe.
    6 June 1655. p 196
    Order that Tho Bacon do work due him, Hagett to put up bond to
    keep the peace. 6 June 1655. p 196
    His dif with Tho Bacon fully settled. He putting away Bacon's
    wife and delivering her goods to her. 6 June 1655. p 197
Haggett, Humph: Sells to Charles Hill 450 acres on S side Rappa. Wit
    Tho x Bacon. Richard x Thompson. 12 Apl 1655. p 207
Haggett, Humphrey. Attachmt agst his estate for debt of - to Mr
    Edmond Kemp. 25 Oct 1655. p 210
Haggett, Humphrie. Attachmt agst him for fees, etc to Vin. Stanford.
    25 Oct 1655. p 211
Haier, Mr Wm. See entry Fra Marsh decd. 7 Aug 1654. p 151
Haines, Morgan. Wit deed Downman to Kinge. 30 Sept 1652. p 120
Haynes, Morgan. With Jno Meriman patents land adj Jno Paine. 26th
    Feb 1653/4. p 183
Haling, Jno. Headright of Capt Hen Fleet. 24 Oct 1653. p 89
Hall, Jenkin. Wit receipt Woodward to Williamson. 4 Dec 1653. p 87
Hall, Jen: To pay levy on 2 tytheables to Mr Ja Williamson. 6 Feby
    1654/5. p 174
Hall, Rich. Wit deed Paine to Killman et als. 6 Oct 1654. p 160
Hall, Willm. To pay levy on 3 tytheables to Mr Smith. 7 Dec 1655.
    p 239
Hamlin, Peeter. Headright of Mr Tho Hawkins. 6 Aug 1655. p 208
Hamper, Tho. To pay levy on 2 tytheables to Mr Tho Bourne. 6 Feby
    1654/5. p 174
    See entry Jno. Ashley. 10 Sept 1654. p 188
    To pay levy on 3 tytheables to Mr Kempe. 7 Dec 1655. p 239
Han, Susan. Headright of Jno Gillet. 6 Oct 1654. p 162
Hannum, Jo. His case vs Tobie Horton to Christmas or next arrival
    of Hannum. 25 Oct 1655. p 210

Hanrauly, Darby. Headright of Capt Hen Fleet. 24 Oct 1653. p 89
Hardinge, Tho. He extremely injured Teage Floyne "with stamping on
  his breast with his foot". Record of 6 Aug 1653. p 61
    Since he wrote 'a fairer hand' he transcribed a challenge for
    Capt Tho Hackett. See entry his name. 8 Aug 1653. p 63
      To pay levy on 1 tytheable to Mr Tho Brice. 6 Feb 1654/5.p 174
Hardinge, Wm. Headright of Jno Weir. 6 Oct 1654. p 162
Hardinge of Northumberland Co. See entry David Fox. 22 Sept 1664.
  Northumberland Co. Records No. 15. p 144
Harford, X'per. Headright of Wm Clapham Jr. 6 June 1654. p 145
Harper, Wm. Wit will of Epa Lawson. Signs with mark. 31 Mar 1652.
  p 34
    To pay levy on 2 tytheables to Mr Row Lawson. 24 Oct 1653.p 90
    To put in security to present Toby Horton at the June Court at
    the house of Majr Jno Carter. 6 Feb 1653/4. p 139
    To give evidence re Toby Horton's londing guns to Indians. 6th
    June 1654. p 146
    Is pd 1000 lb tobo for informing agst Toby Horton who loaned a
    gun to the Indians. 6 Oct 1654. p 164
    To be pd for 1 wolf. 6 Feb 1654/5. p 173
    To pay levy on 3 tytheables to Maj Jno Carter. 6 Feb 1654/5.
    p 174
Harris, Ba-. Headright of Mr Ja Bagnall. 6 Aug 1655. p 208
Haris, Edw. Deceased. Land owned by him adj 88 acres patented by
  Rice Jones on N side Rappa: River. 2 Sept 1652. p 53
Haris, Geo. Assigned 1/2 of 408 acres by Howell Powell. See entry
  Charles Sneade. 12 Jan 1652/3. p 52
  He and Howell Powell assigned 320 acres by Rice Jones. 28 Feb
  1652/3. pp 54-5
Haris, Rog: To pay levy on 3 tytheables to Mr Ja Bagnall. 6th Feby
  1654/5. p 174
Haris, Roger. He and his wife to keep the child of Tho: Mannah and
  Eliz Tomlin till 18. He to have all the tobo from Jno Robinson.
  6 June 1655. p 198
Harrys, Roger. To pay levy on 2 tytheables to Mr Griffin. 7 Dec 1655.
  p 236
Harris, Tho. Headright of Capt Hen Fleet. 24 Oct 1653. p 89
Harris, Wm. P of A dated 14 Jan 1650/1, Wm Harris to Jno Astell. See
  entry Hen Monford. 12 Aug 1650. p 83
  P of A from John Shepheard of Roterdam, merchant, who refers to
  him as "his welbeloved brother Wm Harris". 12 Aug 1650. p 84
Harison, Bour. "Upon the complainte of Tho Meads the Court hath
  ordered that Bour Harison shall serve nine weekes at the Ex-
  pira'con of his time for running away from his said master
  Tho Meads". 7 August 1654. p.152
  I must say that that entry took my breath away for an instant.
  B.F.
Harison, Ha-, and her brother. See entry Wm Neesham. 6 June 1654.
  p 146

Harwood, Elizabeth. Headright of Wm Tigner. 6 Apl 1653. p 43
Harwood, Tho. Gave a heifer to Eliz dau of Jno Meriman prior to 7th
    Aug. 1652. p 8
    Admr of Jno Eaton decd. See entry his name. 8 Dec 1653. p 97
    Patent dated 14 Nov 1649, 300 acres, a neck adj land of John
    Meriman upon a branch of Iland Neck Creek called Grymes Creeke
    in Rappa river, etc.   Tho Harwood sells this land to John
    Sharpe. Wit: Tho Willis. Nicho: Flower. 26 June 1651. p 119
Harwoods Neck. Land sold by Powell to Downman located there. 19 Nov
    1652. p 216
Hathaway see Hadway and Haddaway
Hauker, Mr. To pay levy on 1 tytheable to Mr Tho Brice. 6 Feb 1654/5.
    p 174
Hawker, Mr. To pay levy on 1 tytheable to Wm Neesham. 7 Dec 1655.
    p 237
Hawker, Enoch. Grant to him and Anthony Doney of 1000 acres in Lanc.
    Co., on NW branch of Corotowman. 29 July 1652. p 47
Hauker, Enock. Ordered to pay debt of 930 lb tobo due Wm Clapham Sr.
    6 Oct 1653. p 80
Hauker, Enock. Confesses judgt to Mr Tho Griffen 821 lb tobo. 6 Feb
    1654/5. p 171
Haukins, Mr. To pay levy on 3 tytheables to Mr Jno Catlet. 6th Feb
    1654/5. p 174
Hawkins, Mr. To pay levy on 5 tytheables to Mr Lucas. 7 Dec 1655.
    p 238
Hawkins, Mr Tho. Certificate for land for importing 8 persons. 6th
    Aug 1655. p 208
Hawkins, Mr Tho. (I simply cannot read the entry to follow. Every
    name, in fact every word subject to correction. B.F.) Attachmt
    agst the estate of Wm Veale (this name may even be Wm Smart)
    for 1113 lb tobo due David Lunte. 6 Aug 1655. p 209
Hawkins, Tho. Title to 600 acres to be delivered him by Mr Richerds
    Parratt atty of Tho Lucas. 3 Feb 1654/5. p 218
Hawkins, Tho of Rappa. Assigned 500 acres by Tho Lucas. 3 Feb 1654/5.
    p 218. Also on p 220. In this last entry his name appears as
    Tho Hawkinges.
Hawley, as Orley. See Fox family memo.
Hayward, Syth. Gunner aboard the Rich and Benjamin of London, died
    intestate. Capt John Whittey, Commander of the ship "out of a
    tender care of his widow and orphants" petitions for admr of
    his estate. This is granted. 7 March 1653/4. p 142.
Helliard, Benj. Wit deed of gift Fantleroy to Griffin. 22 Sept 1653.
    p 74. Also on p75. In the second entry the name appears as
    Benjamin Heliard.
Hemings, Augustine. Wit P of A Kempe to Clarke. 9 Sept 1651. p 57
Henshaw, Tho. Headright of Wm Brocas. 6 Oct 1652. p 16
Herd, Walter. Bill to Coll John Carter 1276 lb tobo to be pd 10 Oct
    next. Wit: Edward Dale. Vincent Stanford. 1 Apl 1657. p 130 A.
    This date is as shown in the record and is doubtless correct.
    The item is the first of those out of order in this book. B.F.

Herd, Walter. His name appears as Heard, Hurd, etc. For further
    detail see entries under Conway, Edmonds and Meredith. The
    first item in the first volume of Virginia Colonial Abstracts
    has to do with him. I consider him one of my oldest colonial
    friends and do hope he did not come to the bad end I feared for
    him. B.F.
Hurd, Walter. In regard to the Edmonds estate see entry Edwin Conway.
    6 April 1654. p 140
Herd, Walter. Appointed admr of Mrs Frances Edmonds dec'd, being "her
    own sonne". 7 March 1653/4. p 142
Heard, Walter. See entry Elias Edmonds dec'd. 6 June 1654. p 144
Herd, Walter. Appears as admr of Elias Edmonds dec'd. 7 Aug 1654.
    p 151
Herd, Walter. To be relieved of administration of Elias Edmonds'
    estate. Jno Meredith joint admr. 6 June 1655. p 199
Herd, Walter. Buys 400 acres from Tho and Howell Powell. 19 Oct 1655.
    p 217
Herds, Walter and Elizabeth. Assign to Jno Meredith 300 acres on NE
    side Corotomen River. Wit: Vin Stanford. Tho: Jones. 16 May
    1655. Acknowledged by Tho Powell atty of Eliz Herd and Walter
    Herd 25 Oct 1655. p 227
Herd, Walter. To pay levy to V Stanford. 7 Dec 1655. p 235
Herd's patent with assignment to Jo Meredith with the grant of her
    part to Eliz Greene. 7 Dec 1655. p 231
Hickson, Geo. Headright of Sir H Chisley. 10 Jan 1652/3. p 27 *Jan 10, 1653*
    Signs schedule of Capt Wm Brocas' estate. Recorded 7 May 1655.
    p 191   *Jan 1555*
    Is a servant in the estate of Capt Wm Brocas. "to serve 2 yeares
    and 1/2". 6 June 1655. p 202   *5 p c*
Hill, Charles. Wit P of A dated 14 Jan 1660/1 Harris to Astell. See
    entry Hen Monford. 12 Aug 1650. p 83
Hill, Charles. Buys 450 acres on S side Rappa from Humph Haggett.
    Wit: Tho x Bacon. Richard x Thompson. 12 Apl 1655. p 207
Hill, Jno. Wit deed James to Best. 5 Sept 1654. p 184
Hine, Tho. Headright of Capt Hen Fleet. 24 Oct 1653. p 89
Hobert, Mr (Bertram Obert). To pay levy on 2 tytheables to Mr Richd
    Perrot. 24 Oct 1653. p 93
Hobert, Bartram. His land on Sunderland Creek. 5 Mar 1651/2. p 118
Hobert, Mr Bartram. To view Abra Moone's crop and report damage. 7
    Aug 1654. p 151
Horbartt, Mr Barthr. To appraise est of Capt Wm Brocas decd. 7 May
    1655. p 189
Hobart, Mr Bartram. To view land sold by Moone to Dun. 6 June 1655.
    p 196
Hobart, Bartrum. Signs inv of Capt Wm Brocas' est. 14 May 1655. p 202
Hogkins, Anto. Wit deed Edwards to Ball. 31 Dec 1653. p 149
Hogskins, Bartho. (Hoskins). His land on SW side Gilson's Creek and
    adj land patented by Jno Gillet. 4 Feb 1653/4. p 167
Hokedaye, Wm. (Hookaday). Formerly occupied 600 acres on North side
    Peanckatancke River. See entry Rd Lake 7 Oct 1653. p 109. Also
    entry Rd Lake 5 Oct 1653. p 107

Holdman, Garret. Headright of Danl Welch. 6 Aug 1653. p 62

Holland, Fra: Wit receipt Allen from Perott. See Allen entry. 23rd Oct 1649. p 48

Holliman, Jud: and Epr. (Christopher Holliman). Headrights of John Sherlock. 24 Oct 1653. p 89

Hollis, Jno. Assigned to Abra Moone a debt "long depending". See entry Moone. 6 Aug 1653. p 61

Hollos-, Tho. (practically illegible) Headright of Mr Ja Bagnell. 6 Aug 1655. p 208

Holwell, Tho. Headright of Capt More Fantleroy. 10 Jan 1652/3. p 27

Hopkins, Tho. To pay levy on 4 tytheables to Mr Tho Brice. 6 Febry 1654/5. p 174

    Buys 300 acres "Narow Neck" from Tho Borough. 5 Feb 1654/5. p 180

    To pay levy on 1 tytheable to Wm Neesham. 7 Dec 1655. p 237

Horton, Tobias. Usually entered as Toby Horton.

    1095 lb tobo to be pd at his house next Oct by Tho Seamor to Tho Carter. 16 Mar 1652/3. p 47

    To pay levy on 3 tytheables to Mr Row Lawson. 24 Oct 1653. p 90

    In regard to his lending guns to Indians. A report on this to be made to next Court by Henry Rye, Jno Bunch and Wm Harper. 6 June 1654. p 146

    Case agst him "on behalf of the Lord Protector" refered to. 7 Aug 1654. p 152

    Fined 2000 lb tobo for lending a gun to the Indians. William Harper who informed agst him to have 1000 lb tobo. 6 October 1654. p 164

    Sues Walter Flemminge for debt of 300 lb of tobo "for the cure of a soare leg", the cure not effected. "the Court hath anihillated the said debt and adjudged the said bill cancelled and voyd". 6 Feb 1654/5. p 171

    To pay levy on 3 tytheables to Capt Hen Fleet. 6 Feb 1654/5. p 174

    Sued by Wm Clapham Jr atty of Jas Hannum. Does not appear. 6th June 1655. p 196

    Certificate for land for importing 3 persons. 6 Aug 1655. p 208

    Suit of Wm Clapham vs him to next Court. 6 Aug 1655. p 209

    Arrested at suit of Jo Hannum. Case referred to Christmas or the first arrival of Hannum. 25 Oct 1655. p 210. (Merry Xmas to you, Toby !)

Hoskins. See Hogkins and Hodgskins.

Houle, Nich. To pay levy to V Stanford. 7 Dec 1655. p 235

Howes, Daniell. "Mr Potter I desire you to apeare in Court for me at the house of Mr Lawson against Wm White upon an a'con of debt as by my booke apears as alsoe for a bill of 600 pounds of tobacco and caske pased over by Mr Fox as Mr Fox will witness and Domine who also saw the said bill. alsoe against Wm Wraton for his debt due alsoe on the booke and what yu shall thinke good to doe hearin I shall be contented with and beare yu harmlesse Witness my hand this 26th of May 1653

                                       Daniell howes"

    8 die 10bris 1653. p 87

How, Capt Daniell. His atty Cuth: Potter. 8 Dec 1653. p 97
Howe, Capt Daniell. His atty Cuth: Potter. See entry his name. 30th
     Nov 1653. p 117
Howe, Capt Da. His atty Cuth: Potter to be pf 303 lb tobo by Wm
     Wråughton. 6 Feb 1653/4. p 137
How, Capt Da: Attachmt agst his estate L 100. Sterling for debt due
     Sir Hen Chisley. 7 March 1653/4. p 142
Howma-, Eliz. Headright of Mr Toby Smith. 6 Aug 1655. p 209
Huberd, Hen. Wit receipt Astell to Underwood. 1 Feb 1650/1. p 86
Hugale, Tho. See entry Rd Lake. 7 Oct 1653. p 109
Hughs, An. Headright of Mr Tho Carter. 6 Feb 1654/5. p 172
Hughs, Wm. Headright of Rd Perrott. 10 Jan 1652/3. p 26
Humphreyes, Jno. Wit deed Lake to Kibble. 7 Oct 1653. p 109
Humphreys, Jno. Headright of Mr Tho Hawkins. 6 Aug 1655. p 208
Humfrey, Math: To pay levy on 1 tytheable to Mr Bagnall. 7 Dec 1655.
     p 236
Humphreys. Tho. Headright of Da: Felps. 6 Feb 1653/4. p 139
Humphrey, Tho. Wit deed Meriwether to Hagett. 3 Oct 1654. p 178
Hunt, Jno. To pay Teage Floyne 15 lb tobo having subpoenaed him.
     6 Oct 1652. p 17
     Admr of Geo Eaton. See entry Jno Sharpe. 6 Apl 1653. p 44
     His atty Jno Sharpe. See entry Jno Eaton. 8 Dec 1653. p 97
Hurst, Toby. To appraise est of Tho Meads decd. 6 June 1655. p 197
     To pay levy on 2 tytheables to Mr Wm Underwood. 7 Dec 1655.
     p 234
Husbands, Mr Richd. See entry Abra Weeks. 6 Feb 1653/4. p 137
Hutchins, Wm. Wit deed Meredith to Marsh. 1 Apl 1654. p 134
Hutchins, Elizabeth the wife of Wm Hutchins. Also appears as Eliz
     Greene als Hutchins. See entry Jno Bond concerning her land.
     4 Dec 1655. pp 241-2

Illegible. 1st entry on page 209.
     1st entry on page 213. Has to do with appraisal of certain
     goods. 25 Oct 1655.
Indians. In annual County expenses "to Jesper for his paines
     amongst the Indyans when Taweeran was kild 0150 lb tobo".
     24 Oct 1653. p 95 (Note: My impression is that this was Jesper
     Griffin who was connected in smme way with Capt Hen Fleet. BF)
     In regard to trespasses by the Wickocomikoes see entry Henry
     Fleet. 6 June 1655. p 198
     They to be allowed 80 lb tobo for each wolf's head brought in.
     25 Oct 1655. p 210
     Indian Cabins in Fleets Bay. 1 Aug 1652. p 132
Ingram, Jno. Wit Lylly to Keegam and Pine. 7 Sept 1652. p 40
Ingram, Tobyas. Wit mortgage Lambertson to Wm'son. 31 Jan 1653/4.
     p 136
Ireland, Wm. To pay levy on 3 tytheables to Mr Geo Taylor. 6 Feby
     1654/5. p 174

Island Neck. On N side Rappa near Corotomen. See Newsam et als. 29
    Jan 1649/50. p 69
Iland Neck Creek. Called Grymes Creek. See entry Tho Harwood. 14th
    Nov 1649. p 119

Jackman, Mr Antho. Appointed Constable for S side of Rappahannock
    river. He to repair to the next Comm'r of the Quorum he shall
    live by, ie Mr Jas Bagnall. 6 Aug 1652. p 3
    Is sued by Jno Edgecomb for land sold him. 6 Oct 1652. p 15
    Grant of 550 acres in Rappa abt 37 miles on the N side, adjs
    Jackmans Creek, land of Capt More Fantleroy. No date shown
    for the grant. This land assigned to Jno Edgecomb 6 Oct 1652.
    Wit: Edwin Conaway. John Phillips. Recorded 29 Dec 1652. p 19
    Gives bill 3000 lb tobo to Rd Bennett mercht. Wit Ric: Loes.
    4 June 1652. p 20
    Buys 260 acres on S side Rappa from Rd Bennett. Land adj Rich.
    Loes, etc. Wit W Claiborne. Ric: Loes. 4 June 1652. p 22
    Judgt to him agst Mrs Luc'e Marsh for 250 lb tobo. 6 Apl 1653.
    p 44
    His land adjs that sold by Bennett to Loes. 4 June 1652. p 46
    To pay levy on 2 tytheables to Mr Jas Bagnall. 24 Oct 1653.
    p 94
    He owes 670 lb tobo by bill to est of Robt Vivian decd. 10th
    Feb 1653/4. p 117
    To pay levy on 2 tytheables to Mr Ja Bagnall. 6 Feb 1654/5.
    p 174
    His a/c included in settlemt of Lawson est. 20 Jan 1655/6.
    p 192.
    To pay Wm Johnson admr to Paule Brewer decd 575 lb tobo. 25th
    Oct 1655. p 211
    Com of admr to him on est of Christopher Werne. 7 Dec 1655.
    p 232
    To pay levy on 3 tytheables to Mr Bagnall. 7 Dec 1655. p 236
Jackson, Jno. Wit deed Moone to Bourne. 26 May 1652. p 106
James, Edward. Grant. 4 Jan 1653/4. 350 acres abt 39 miles up on N
    side Rappa, adj Willinge Creek, New Haven Creek.
    James assigns above to Tho Best 5 Sept 1654. Wit: Tho Newman.
    John Hill.
    Best assigns his interest to Tho Wms and Alexander Porteus 6th
    Feb 1654/5. Wit Tho: Madestard. Vinc Stanford.   pp 184-5.
James, Edward. Sells Tho Best and Xp'er Aschley 350 acres betw two
    creeks, Jackmans and Folly. Wit. Tho Godwin. Dated 28 August
    1651, which is prob an error, the date prob being 1654.
    Best assigns above to Tho Wms and Alexander Porteus 6th Feb
    1654/5. Wit Tho Madestard. Vincent Stanford.   p 185
James, Wm. Headright of Fra Gower. 8 Dec 1653. p 96
Jarins, Sarah. Headright of Tho Griffin. 10 Jan 1652/3. p 24

Jefrys, Jno. Citizen and Grocer of London. P of A to Coll Rich Lee
   of Virginia Esqr to transact business. Wit: Sam Chew. Hugh
   Wilson. Tho: Bowler. Sam Cooper. 7 Feb 1652/3. p 112
Jeffryes, Jno. Sued Mr Conaway for L 19. 16. 0 Sterling, who not
   appearing, judgt agst Jno Phillips the Sheriff. 6 Apl 1654.
   p 141
Jefferyes, Jno. His atty Abra Moone in dif with Mr Edwin Conaway.
   6 Feb 1654/5. p 173
Jenkinson, Fra. Headright of Rd Perrott. 10 Jan 1652/3. p 26
Jennings, Jno. Wit assignmt of land Lucas to Hawkins. 3 Feb 1654/5.
   p 218. Also on p 220
Jesper. See entry Indians. 24 Oct 1653. p 95 (Jesper Griffin)
Johnson, Daniell. Headright of Oliver Segar. 6 Aug 1653. p 62
Jonson, Dorick. Headright of Epe Boney. 10 Jan 1652/3. p 26
Jonson, Jno. Buys 200 acres on Sunderland Creek from Hen Nicholls.
   25 Apl 1653. p 157
   Confesses judgt to Maj Tho Curtis for 500 lb tobo with 2 yrs
   interest. 6 Oct 1654. p 163
Johnson, Jo. On his petition for himself and his brothers and sis-
   ters, Robt Burton is admitted guardian for them. Comm of admr
   to Burton (does not state whose estate). Mr Obert and Mr
   Wyllis to appraise est. Wm Copeland security. 7 Dec 1655.p 231
Jonson, Will. Wit bond Dedman to Bennett. 4 June 1652. p 4
Jonson, Wm. Certificate for 50 acres for importing Frances Coulstone.
   6 Oct 1652. p 15
Jonson, Wm. Wit deed Bennett to Dedman. 4 June 1652. p 21
Jonson, Wm. Swears regarding bequest Dandridge to Lawson. .10 Jan
   1652/3. p 25
Jonson, Wm. Nonsuit to him at suit of Rich Perott. 10 Jan 1652/3.
   p 27
Jonson, Wm. His daughter Ann Jonson given 5 hogs by Hen Dedman now
   exchanged for a red cow. 19 Jan 1652/3. p 30
Johnson, Wm. Owes wages for a servant to Mr Richd Parett. 24 Febry
   1652/3. p 45
Jonson, Wm. Dif betw him and Peeter Taylor to next Court. 6th Oct
   1653. p 78
Johnson, Wm. To pay levy on 2 tytheables to Mr Jas Bagnall. 24 Oct
   1653. p 94
Jnoson, Wm. To pay levy on 2 tytheables to Mr And Gilson. 6th Feby
   1654/5. p 174
Johnson, Wm. His a/c and that of Daniell Jonson included in settle-
   ment of Mr Epa Lawson's estate. 20 Jan 1655/6. p 192
Johnston, Wm. Admr of estate of Paul Brewer to him. 6 June 1655.
   p 196
Johnson, Wm. Assigned debt 700 lb tobo to Mr Tho Griffin agst est
   of Paul Brewer. 6 June 1655. p 197
Johnson, Wm. To admr est of Paul Brewer if Mr Jno Cox fails in proof.
   6 June 1655. p 201
Jonson, Wm. 400 lb tobo to have been pd Mr Robt Pitt for his use by
   Mr Epa Lawson decd. 6 June 1655. p 201

Johnson, Wm. Admr of est of Paule Brewer decd. 25 Oct 1655. p 211

Johnson, Wm. Assigns John Gregory all interest "in this pattente". Does not give other detail. Wit: Richerd Loes. Tho Greefeth. 14 Aug 1654. p 218

Johnson, Willm. To pay levy on 3 tytheables to Mr Smith. 7 Dec 1655. p 239

Jollins, Wm of Cherry Point, Northumberland Co and Rebecca his wife. See Fox family memo.

Jones, Mr. To pay levy on 4 tytheables to Mr Jas Bagnell. 24th Oct 1653. p 94

Jones, Mr. To pay levy on 4 tytheables to Mr Ja Bagnall. 6th Feby 1654/5. p 174

Jones, Da: (Daniel) To put in security to appear at next Court re Domine Theriott. 7 Aug 1654. p 152

Jones, Daniel. Informs that Wm Denby delivered a gun to an Indian. 6 Oct 1654. p 163

Attachmt agst his est to Tho Roots for debt of 300 lb tobo. 6th Feb 1654/5. p 173

Jones, Hugh. Headright of David Fox. 6 Oct 1652. p 15

Headright of Wm Tigner. 6 Apl 1653. p 43

Jones, Rice. Certificate for 200 acres for transporting 4 persons. 6 Aug 1652. p 2

Appears as of Rappahannock in bond to Richd Bennett mercht for 12000 lb tobo. Wit: Wm Clayborne. Tho: Brice. 7 June 1652. p 6

Buys abt 600 or 700 acres, part of a patent of 4 Nov 1642 from Richd Bennett mercht. 7 June 1652. p 8

His suit vs Wm Wratton dismissed. 10 Jan 1652/3. p 24

Ordered to pay corn, clothes etc to John Bell, he having finished his time. 10 Jan 1652/3. p 24

As of Virginia, planter, sells Evan Petterson 350 acres known as Muskeeto poynt 22 Oct 1652. Wit: Tho Rootes. Tho Littlepage. Also in the presence of Tho: Madestard. Tho: Littlepage. This land is now sold by Walter Bruce attorney of Ever Petterson to Ebber Baning. Wit: Cornelius Oudlantt. Charls Rawlins. Wm Batte. 29 Oct 1652. p 39

As of Rappahannock River. Sells Howell Powell of the same place planter, 408 acres, made up of 2 patents, 320 acres in one and 88 in the other. On N side Rappa adj land of Wm Newsome. Wit: Edwin Conaway. Geo Sleight. Dated 8 Jan 1652. Recorded 6 Apl 1653. p 51

Wit: Powell to Haris. 12 Jan 1652/3. p 52

Patents 88 acres in Lancaster Co on N side Rappa, adj land of Edw Haris decd 2 Sept 1652. This land assigned by Jones to Howell Powell 22 Jan 1652/3. Wit Edwin Conawaye. p 53

Wit: Coleman to Mascall. No date shown. Prior to 1653. pp 54-5

Assigns interest in 320 acres to Howell Powell and Geo Harris. 28 Feb 1652/3. pp 54-5

Ordered to pay a debt of 1053 lb tobo to Abra Moone attorney of Coll Rich Lee Esqr. 6 Feb 1653/4. p 138

Jones, Rice. Judgt agst him as security for Wm Catten 260 lb tobo
to Wm Wraughton. 6 June 1654. p 146
His property, formerly belonging to Rd Bennett on boundry line
of 2 parishes now formed. 7 Aug 1654. p 152
To appraise est of Tho Steephens decd. 7 Aug 1654. p 153
Wit Browne to Clapham Sr (as Rice RI Jones). 6 June 1655.
p 195
Jones, Richd. To pay levy on 2 tytheables to Mr Bagnall. 7 Dec 1655.
p 236
Jones, Tho. Wit Herd to Meredith. 16 May 1655. p 227

Keale, Geo. Headright of Jno Gillet. 6 Oct 1654. p 162
Keds, Tho. Assigns land to Thos Pattison. Does not show location.
Wit: Thos Willis. Richard Leavan. 8 Oct 1655. p 219
Keds, Thomas of Lancaster Co, planter, sells Tho Pattison and Richd
Bridges of same Co, 200 acres for 1700 lb tobo. This land on S
side Rappa and on NW side of SW branch of Burnams Creek and
adjs land of Robt Chowninge, etc. Wit: Arther Dune. Tho Willis.
16 Apl 1655. p 219
Keeble see Kible.
Keegam, Will. Buys land with Jno Pine from Edwd Lilly. 7 Sept 1652.
p 40
Kemp, Ann. Headright of Mr Edmond Kemp. 25 Oct 1655. p 213
Kempe, Bridgett of the parish of Sepney alias Stevenheath in the Co
of Middlesex, widow. Power of Atty to well beloved friend
Daniell Clarke "of the Iland of Virginia", planter, to collect
debts now due in Virginia. Wit: Augustine Hemings. Thomas
Mitchell. Steephen Kemp. Dated 9 Sept 1651. p 57
Kempe, Mr. (Edmond) To pay levy on 16 tytheables to Mr Jno Cox. 24
Oct 1653. p 93
Kempe, Edmond of Rappa River in Lanc Co buys 600 acres from George
Reade on - side of Peacketanke River. 16 May 1654. p 159
To appraise est of Rd Lake decd. 6 Oct 1654. p 162
To pay levy on 5 tytheables to Mr Jno Cox. 6 Feb 1654/5. p 174
To appraise est of Capt Wm Brocas decd. 7 May 1655. p 189
Justice. 7 May 1655. p 189
To inquire into Hagett - Bacon situation. See entries their
names. 6 June 1655. p 196
Signs inv Brocas estate. 14 May 1655. p 202
Justice. 25 Oct 1655. p 210
The market place for Peanke River to begin at Mr Kemp's and
run 10 miles upwards. 25 Oct 1655. p 210
Attachmt agst Humphrey Haggett's est for debt of - lb tobo due
by bill. 25 Oct 1655. p 210
He and Tho Griffith to pay fees Coupland vs Kemp. 25 Oct 1655.
p 211
Certificate for transporting 4 persons. Ann Kemp, Sary Greene,
Marie Sallivan, Daniell an Irish Boy. 25 Oct 1655. p 213
To receive levy on 28 tytheables from 9 persons incl 5 tyth-
eables for himself. 7 Dec 1655. p 239

Kemp, Stephen. Wit P of A from Mrs Bridgett Kempe to Danl Clarke.
9 Sept 1651. p 57
Keys, Sarah. Headright of Rd Perrott. 6 Oct 1653. p 77
Kibble, Geo., planter of Gloucester Co. Buys 200 acres on N side of
Peanoketanoke River from Rd. Lake. See entry his name. Adjs
land of Peeter Rigby, etc. 7 Oct 1653. p 109
To admr est of Rd Lake as greatest creditor. 6 Oct 1654. p 162
As admr of Rd Lake dec'd to pay 465 lb tobo to Mr Toby Smith
atty of Capt Jno Whitty. 6 Oct 1654. p 163
Appears as admr of Rd Lake decd. 6 Feb 1654/5. p 173
To pay levy on 3 tytheables to Mr Tho Bourne. 6 Feb 1654/5
p 174
Judgt agt him as admr of Rd Lake decd to Mr Toby Smith atty of
Capt Jno Whitty for 1016 lb of "bisquite". 6 June 1655. p 198
To have 'an quitus est', he having pd beyond the assets. Does
not show what estate. 25 Oct 1655. p 211
To pay levy on 2 tytheables to Mr Kempe. 7 Dec 1655. p 239
Kid, Tho. To pay levy on 3 tytheables to Mr Rd Perrot. 24 Oct 1653.
p 93
To pay levy on 3 tytheables to Mr Rd Perrott. 6 Feb 1654/5.
p 174
To view land sold by Moone to Dun. 6 June 1655. p 196
To pay levy on 3 tytheables to Abra Weekes. 7 Dec 1655. p 237
Killman, John and George and Tho For- (possibly Forest) buy 250
acres on S side Rappa up Coxe's Creek from Ralph Paine. 6th
Oct 1654. p 160
To pay levy on 3 tytheables to Mr Smith. 7 Dec 1655. p 239
Kinge, Charles. Buys Downman's interest in 300 acres owned by Edw
Dudley, Wm Downman and Ben Powell. 30 Sept 1652. p 120
Administration of est of Robt Perfect decd, he having married
the relict. Tho Powell security. 6 June 1654. p 146
To pay levy on 1 tytheable to Mr Tho Brice. 6 Feb 1654/5.p 174
To pay levy on 1 tytheable to Wm Neesham. 7 Dec 1655. p 237
Kinge, Richd. Servant to Epa Lawson. 13 Apl 1651. p 9
Was servt to Epa: Lawson decd. To serve 2 yrs. 2 June 1652.
2 June 1652. p 10
Kingman, Hen. Headright of David Fox. 6 Oct 1652. p 15
Kinsey, Mr. To pay levy to V Stanford. 7 Dec 1655. p 235
Kinsey, Paull. Wit deed Powell to Herd. 19 Oct 1655. p 217
Kitchin, Wm. Deceased. Admr of his est to Wm Clapham Jr. 6 Apl 1653.
p 43
Knight, Peet'r. Wit deed Roots to Grimes. 8 Dec 1653. p 122
Knight, Salter. Headright of Wm Clapham Sr. 6 Oct 1652. p 15
Knopp, Robt. Having absented himself from his master, Geo Beach, is
ordered to serve him 6 months longer. 7 Dec 1655. p 231. (Note:
Bad idea. Not original with me. Having absented myself from
Va. Colonial Abstracts for a 6 months spree on the Gulf of
Mexico, now find I must serve the balance of my life, producing
abstracts of Westmoreland, York and Lower Norfolk Counties. BF)

Lacye, Jno. Headright of Sir H Chisley. 10 Jan 1652/3. p 27
Lake, Rich: of Lancaster Co. Sells Peeter Rigby of Glocerster Co.,
    planter, 400 acres, part of 600 acres in Mr Jno Mottrom's name
    on N side of Peancketanok River, adj land formerly occupied by
    Wm Hockaday, etc.. Wit: Row Haddaway. Jno Needles. 5th Octbr.
    1653. p 107
Lake, Rich: of Gloucester Co., sells Geo Kibble of same Co., planter,
    200 acres, part of 600 acres on N side of Peanceketancke River,
    adj land formerly occupied by Wm Hookedaye and the 400 acres
    now in occupation of Peeter Rigby, Hen Forrett and Tho Hugate.
    Wit: John Humphreys. Jno Smither. 7 Oct 1653. p 109
Lake, Rich. Wit deed Bonner to Tignor. 6 June 1654. p 147
Lake, Richard, deceased. Admr of his est to Geo Kibble the greatest
    creditor. Tho Bourne and Edmd Kemp appraisers. Mr Jno Cox to
    admr the oath. Rowland Hadaway and his wife to deliver up the
    est on oath. 6 Oct 1654. p 162
    Judgt to Mr Toby Smith atty of Capt Jno Whitty agst his est
    for 465 lb tobo to be pd by Geo Kibble admr. 6 Oct 1654. p 163
    Judgt agst his est to Abra Moone 600 lb tobo on testimony of
    Geo Waddings to be pd by Geo Kibble admr. 6 Oct 1654. p 164
    His admr, Geo Kibble, ordered to pay debt of 1302blb tobo to
    Capt Hen Fleet. 6 Feb 1654/5. p 173
    His admr ordered to pay judgt for 1300 lb tobo to Abr Moone.
    6 Feb 1654/5. p 173
    Judgt agt his admr, Geo Kibble, to Mr Toby Smith atty of Capt
    Jno Whitty for 1016 lb of 'Bisquitt'. 6 June 1655. p 198
    Judgt agt his est 112 lb tobo to Mr Peeter Rigbey. 6 June 1655.
    p 198
    Wit P of A Whitty to Smith. 19 May 1654. p 222
Lambert, Mr. To pay levy on 12 tytheables to Mr Da: Fox. 24 Oct 1653.
    p 91
    To pay levy on 5 tytheables to Mr Ja Williamson. 6 Feb 1654/5.
    p 174
Lamberson, Lambert. Confesses judgt 3400 lb tobo to Mr David Fox.
    10 Jan 1652/3. p 23
    Judgt to him agt Teage Floyne for 400 lb tobo for cure for
    being hurt. To be pd 10 Nov. 6 Aug 1653. p 61
    Mortgages 3 cows and half of 3 servants now in possession of
    Tho Meader to Ja Williamson. Wit: Chresto Brownrigge. Tobyas
    Ingram. 31 Jan 1653/4. p 136
    A letter. "Mr Smyth my service presented Sir I am indebted to
    Mr Wm'son and hath pased my specialtye my oeasions will not let
    me come to the Court to acknowledge it therfore I wrote this to
    testefye under my hand that it is my Act and seale and I do
    acknowledge the same in Court under my hand Janry the 31th
    1653   Lambert Lambertson". (1653/4) p 135
    Attachmt agst his estate at suit of L Col An: Elliott attorney
    of Tho Purifye for 4500 lb tobo on action of non inv est. 6th
    Feb 1653/4. p 138
    To pay levy on 5 tytheables to Mr Wm Underwood. 7 Dec 1655.
    p 234

Lampkin, Thos Certificate for land for importing 1 person, Elinor
   Lusher (?). 6 Oct 1653. p 79
Langford, Tho. Headright of V Stanford. 6 June 1655. p 198
Lanman, Jno. His land in Rappa River adj Brecknock Bay and land
   patented by Jno Godwin. 22 May 1650. p 168
Lasinbey. Jno. Headright of Mr Rich Leake. 6 Feb 1653/4. p 139
Laud, Tho. (or Land). Headright of Capt Hen Fleet. 24 Oct 1653.
   p 89
Lawrence, Mr. In annual County expense "To Major Jo: Carter per ord
   for Mr Lawrence charges Ao 1651 1090 lb tobo". 24 Oct 1653.p 95
Laws. Order "for the whole book of acts in force". 6 Feb 1654/5.
   p 172. Also see entry Mr Edw Dale. 7 Dec 1655. p 240
Lawson, Mr. Cuthbert Potter to appear for Danl Howes when Court is
   held "at the house of Mr Lawson". 26 May 1653. p 87
Lawson, Elizabeth daughter of Mr Epa Lawson deceased. See entry Rd
   Bennett. 12 Sept 1652. p 31
Lawson, Epaproditus. A bond to protect Richd Bennett from a debt of
   40000 lb tobo due Symon Cuerzee which Bennett stands bound for.
   Security land with 6 servants named Daniell Diskey, Jno Cooke,
   Richard Kinge, Francis -, Margarett -, -. Also debts: L 22. 7.
   due from Mr Fra Gyles and L 10. Sterling due from Capt Thomas
   Richards. Wit: Christopher Willoughbey. John Seapes. 13 April
   1651. p 9
   His inventory. 2 June 1652. p 10
Lawson, Epaphroditus. Deceased. His estate appraised by Col Thomas
   Burbage and Major Jno Billingsby. It includes 4 servants: Thos
   Maydstone for 2 yrs at 1200 lb tobo, Richard Kinge for 3 yrs
   (2 yrs) at 1200 lb tobo, John Cooke for 3 yrs at 1600 lb
   tobo, Margarett Maloy 1/2 yr at 100 lb tobo. Also 64 books
   small and greate at 300 lb tobo. 2 June 1652. p 10
   Admr of his est to Dominick Therriott to pay debt 3400 lb tobo.
   6 Oct 1652. p 16
   His relict married Wm Clapham Jr. 6 Oct 1652. p 16
   Admr of his est to Mr Jno Carter for debt 7067 lb tobo. He to
   deliver balance to Domino Theriott. 10 Jan 1652/3. p 23
   His est owes Jno Cornelis 1095 lb tobo. 10 Jan 1652/3. p 24
   His admr ordered to pay 7000 lb tobo he rec'd from estate of
   Elis Dandridge dec'd for use of Rowland the son of Rowland
   Lawson. Mr Rowland Lawson Sr and Wm Jonson swear to this. 10th
   Jan 1652/3. p 25
   His admrs ordered to pay a debt of 800 lb tobo due to Mr Row:
   Lawson. 10 Jan 1652/3. p 25
   He owed Mr Jas Williamson rights for 550 acres. 10 Jan 1652/3.
   p 27
   See entry Rd. Bennett. 12 Sept 1652. p 31
   Patented 700 acres on N side abt 12 miles up on E side of
   Slaughters Creek, which parts the land from that of Jno Carter,
   etc. 3 Sept 1649. p 33
   Patented 2000 acres in Rappa on S side on lowermost point of
   a great Ileland crossing Lawson's Creek, etc. 22 May 1650.p 33

Lawson, Epaphroditas. Will. Dated 31 March 1652. Probated 12 Janry
    1652/3. "I make and ordaigne the Child that my wife now goeth
    with my heir". Wife to have her thirds. Admrs: Mr Rich Bennett
    and Mr John Carter. Wit: Eliz Loes, John x Lee, Wm x Harper.
    p 34
    Patented 1000 acres in Rappa abt 10 miles on N side adj land
    of John Slaughter, etc. 22 Feb 1650/1. p 34
    His estate sued for 3400 lb tobo by Robt Mascall. See involved
    entry in his name. 6 Aug 1653. p 62
    His admrs ordered to pay debt 595 lb tobo due Mr Jno Cox. 6th
    Oct 1653. p 77
    His admrs ordered to pay debt of 3000 lb tobo due Mr Tho Griffin
    assignee of Rich: Lewis. 6 Oct 1653. p 79
    Order that his admr, Mr Jno Carter, be pd 2000 lb tobo from
    this year's levy due for his burgesses charge for 1652. 6th
    Oct 1653. p 79
    Judgt agst his estate for 8431 lb tobo and a 3 yr old steer to
    Rich Richardson attorney of Sym Cuerzee. 8 Dec 1653. p 96
    His exor, Wm Clapham Jr., ordered to pay 690 lb tobo to Mr Tho
    Carter. 6 Feb 1653/4. p 137
    See entry Maj Jno Carter. 6 June 1654. p 145
    See entry Edw Boswell. 6 June 1654. p 146
    An a/c of his estate signed Jno Carter. The following names
    appear in lists of debts, etc. Capt Wormleye, Wm Jnoson and
    Daniell Jonson, Andrew Dower, Mr Loes, Mr Jackman, George
    Raules, Jno Edgcomb, Mr Mead, Mr Wm Clapham Jr., Mr Wm'son,
    Mr To Smyth, Mr Rowland Lawson, Capt Fantleroy, Samuel
    Firment, Peeter Taylor, Jno Sherlock. 20 Jan 1655/6. p 192
    All a/cs of his est settled by Major Jno Carter the admr. 6th
    June 1655. p 199
    He had obliged himself to pay Mr Robt Pitt for the use of Wm
    Jonson abt 400 lb tobo, etc. 6 June 1655. p 201
    He had formerly bought 700 acres from Mr Rd Bennett Esq and
    sold it to Wm Clapham. 30 June 1655. p 229
Lawson, Richd. See entry Rd Bennett. 12 Sept 1652. p 31
    To appraise the est of Robt Chambers decd. 6 Apl 1654. p 140
    To pay levy on 6 tytheables to Mr Jno Catlet. 6 Feb 1654/5.
    p 174
    He is a brother to Row Lawson. 6 June 1655. p 205
    To pay levy on 5 tytheables to Mr Lucas. 7 Dec 1655. p 238
Lawson, Mr Rowland. Justice. 6 Aug 1652. p 2
    Justice. 6 Apl 1653. p 43
    Justice. 6 Aug 1653. p 61
    See entry 'Muster'. 8 Aug 1653. p 65
    To collect levy from E side Costatawmen river downward by the
    side of Rappa on 67 tytheables. 24 Oct 1653. p 90
    Justice. 16 May 1654. p 131
    Justice. 6 Feb 1653/4. p 137
    Security for Da: Grisley. 6 Feb 1653/4. p 138
    Justice. 7 March 1653/4. p 142

Lawson, Mr Rowland. Justice. 6 June 1654. p 144
    Justice. 6 Feb 1654/5. p 171
    Certificate for transportation of 10 persons. 6 Feb 1654/5.
    p 172
    To pay levy on 3 tytheables to Maj Jno Carter. 6 Feb 1654/5.
    p 174
    Justice. 7 May 1655. p 189
    His a/c incl in settlemt of Epa Lawson est. 20 Jan 1655/6. p 192
    Justice. 6 June 1655. p 196
    Patents 400 acres on Rappa adj Geo Eaton, etc. 8 Oct 1655. He
    assigns this land to his brother Mr Rich Lawson. Wit Jno Weir.
    Jno Sharpe. p 205
    Justice. 25 Oct 1655. p 210. His first name appears in this
    entry as 'Roland'.
    Wit P of A Whitty to Smith. 19 May 1654. p 222
    Justice. 7 Dec 1655. p 231
Lea, Wm of parish of St Clements Danes in County of Middlesex,
    broker. Power of Atty to "Loveinge friend" Mr Wm Sheares of
    London, merchant, to settle a/c with James Williamson of
    Redpoynt in Ile of Weight Co in Virginia, gent. Wit: Wm
    Geery. Oliver Geery. Judeth Butterworth. 20 Sept 1649. p 5
Lea, Wm. See entry Tho Whettell. 11 May 1651. p 6
Leake, Mr. To pay levy on 2 tytheables to Mr Tho Bearn. 24 Oct 1653.
    p 92
Leake, Mr Rich: Certificate for transportation of 5 persons. Himself
    twice, Edw Steephenson twice, Jno Lasinbey. 6 Feb 1653/4. p 139
Leavan, Richd. Wit assignmt of land Keds to Pattison. 8 Oct 1655.
    p 219
Le Breton see Britten
Lee, Bridges. Headright of Capt Hen Fleet. 6 June 1655. p 198
Lee, Hen: deceased. His relict married Dominick Thoriott who has
    com of admr of his estate. 10 Jan 1652/3. p 23
    Order that Tho Roots refund 100 lb tobo to his relict Joane
    Lee. 10 Jan 1652/3. p 26
    Dom: Theriott his admr. See entry Abra Moone. 6 Aug 1653. p 61
    Inventory of his est. Total val 5080 lb tobo. Appraised by Edw
    Grimes and Wm Neesham. At end of the list "2 heifers marked
    and given to the Children by Hen Lee in his life time". 7 Mar
    1652/3. p 126
Lee, Humphrey. 600 lb tobo collected from him by Tho Walker for Wm
    Price. 6 June 1655. p 200
Lee, Jno. Wit will of Epa Lawson. Signs with mark. 31 Mar 1652. p 34
Lee, Col. Richard. Payment made by Mr Jas Williamson of 1919 lb tobo
    to John Woodward for Col Lee due on 2 bills assigned by Mr
    Richd Webster of Jamestowne to him. 4 Dec 1653. p 87
    To pay levy on 10 tytheables to Mr Jno Cox. 24 Oct 1653. p 93
    Power of Atty from Jno Jefrys Citizen and Grocer of London. 7th
    Feb 1652/3. p 112
    His atty Abra Moone collects 1053 lb tobo from Rice Jones. 7th
    Feb 1653/4. p 138

Leech, Wm. Wit deed Moone to Allison. 18 Oct 1653. p 103
    To pay levy on 12 tytheables to Mr Jno Cox. 6 Feb 1654/5. p 174
    To appraise est of Capt Wm Brocas decd. 7 May 1655. p 189
    Signs inv of Capt Brocas' est. 14 May 1655. p 202
    To collect levy on 52 tytheables from 8 persons, incl 10
    tytheables for himself. 7 Dec 1655. p 236
Levy. 6 Feb 1654/5. p 174. The following paid levy on 10 or more
    tytheables in their families, which of course included men
    servants.

Major Jno Carter	12
Capt Hen Fleete	11
Mr David Fox	16
Jno Sharpe	14
Rowland Burnham	12
Sir Hen Chicheley	24
Capt Wm Brocas Esqr	12
Lady Eliz Lunsford	12

Lewcas, Mr. (Lucas) To pay levy on 4 tytheables to Mr Jno Catlet.
    6 Feb 1654/5. p 174
Lucas, Mr. To collect levy on 24 tytheables from 6 persons incl 4
    tytheables of his own family. 7 Dec 1655. p 238
Lucas, Tho: P of A to Mr Richerds Parratt of Rappa to deliver in
    Court rights and title of 2 patents of 600 acres to Tho Hawkins
    of Rappa. Wit Tho Lucas Jr. Will Peirse. 3 Feb 1654/5. p 218
Lucas, Tho of Rappahannock assigns Tho Hawkins of Rappa: title in
    500 acres. Does not give location. Wit: John Cattlett. John
    Jennings. 3 Feb 1654/5. p 218. Recognit in Lanc 26 8ber 1655.
Lucas, Tho. of Rappa. Assigns to Tho Hawkinges of Rappa title in 600
    acres. Wit: John Cattlett. John Jenings. 3 Feb 1654/5. p 220
Lucas, Tho. Patent. 600 acres in the Freshes on S side Rappa river
    adj land of Jo Cattlett and Ralfe Rowsee, W on Capt Linche's,
    etc. Dated 7 Aug 165- (blotted-prior to 1654). Sig William
    Barckeley. p 220
Lucas, Thos. Patent. 600 acres on N side Rappa River above the first
    "cliftes", W along "pepeticke" creek, etc. Signed Ri Bennett.
    Will Claiborne. 7 June 1652. p 221
Lucas, Mr Thomas. Justice. 6 Jan 1655/6. p 244
Lucas, Tho Jr. See entry Tho Lucas. 3 Feb 1654/5. p 218
Lewcas, Wm. To pay levy on 2 tytheables to Mr Jno Cox. 6 Feb 1654/5
    p 174
Lucas, Willm. To pay levy on 2 tytheables to Wm Leech. 7 Dec 1655.
    p 236
Lewis, Rich: He assigned a debt of 3000 lb tobo to Tho Griffin due
    from est of Epa Lawson decd. 6 Oct 1653. p 79
    To pay levy on 2 tytheables to Mr Rd Perrot. 24 Oct 1653. p 93
    Patent. 300 acres on S side Rappa river at head of Bartram
    Obert's land and adj a path going to the hind of Nyemcock
    Creek, etc. 29 Nov 1652. p 155. Lewis assigns this land to Mr
    Tho Willis and Richd Watkins 4 Jan 1653/4. Wit: Wm Garber, Em
    Davids. Also a second deed from Lewis to Willis and Watkins
    dated 7 Aug 1654. Wit: John Catlett. Hen Nicholls. p 155

Lewis, Rich. To pay levy on 3 tytheables to Mr Rd Perrott. 6th Feby
    1654/5. p 174
    His land on Sunderland Creek adjs that sold by Welch to Coop-
    land. 6 June 1655. p 194
    To pay levy on 2 tytheable to Abra Weekes. 7 Dec 1655. p 237
Lewis, Robt. Wit: deed Pettibone to Cox. 1 Dec 1655. p 224
Lilly, Edw. (here as Lylly). To have land from Tho Eeevns. See entry
    his name. 7 March 1652/3. p 36
    Assigns all interest in within patent (does not show what
    patent) to Will Keegam and John Pine "dwelling upon Rapahanook".
    Wit: Samuell Gooch. John Ingram. 7 Sept (1652). p 40
Lilley, Jno. His land on S side Mulford Haven adj grant 500 acres
    to Abra Moone. 6 June 1650. p 106
Linche, James. A specialty of his to be delivered to Robt Mascall.
    See entry his name. 6 Aug 1653. p 62
Lindsey, Hugh (appears here as Howgh Lensey). Wit deed Powell to
    Herd. 19 Oct 1655. p 217
Linell, Wm of Lanc Co, planter. Wm Nicholls mortages a cow called
    Naughtie to him for 1000 lb tobo. 30 Nov 1653. p 105
Liner, Silvester (this name open to question). Headright of Epe
    Boney. 10 Jan 1652/3. p 26
Littlepage, Tho. Wit Rice Jones to Petterson. 22 Oct 1652. p 39
    Agrees not to dispose of his crop till Jno Cox is pd. Wit: Hum
    Haggett. Edwd Britten. 16 Jan 1653/4. p 104
Loes, Eliz: Wit will Epa Lawson. 31 March 1652. p 34
Loes, Rich: Wit bond Dedman to Bennett. 4 June 1652. p 4
        Justice. 6 Oct 1652. p 15
    Confesses judgt to Capt Heh Fleet for 1120 lb tobo with one
    year's interest. 6 Oct 1652. p 16
    Signs bill 5580 lb tobo to Rd Bennett mercht. Wit: W Claiborne.
    4 June 1652. p 19
    His land adjs that Rd Bennett sells to Antho Jackman. He wit
    the deed. 4 June 1652. p 22
    Justice. 6 Apl 1653. p 43
    Buys 300 acres from Rd Bennett mercht. See entry his name. 4th
    June 1652. p 46
    Records a heifer given by him and Mr Toby Smith to "Henry
    Wm'son sun in Law to the said Mr Loes". Recorded 6 Aug 1653.
    p 58
    Justice. 6 Aug 1653. p 61
    Justice. 6 Oct 1653. p 77
    To pay levy on 3 tytheables to Mr Jas Bagnall. 24 Oct 1653.
    p 94
    Justice. 8 Dec 1653. p 96
    Wit: deed Underwood to Meads. 12 Sept 1653. p 111
    Wit deed Smyth to Webb. 6 Feb 1653/4. p 128
    Justice. 6 Feb 1653/4. p 137
    Justice. 7 Aug 1654. p 151
    Justice. 6 Feb 1654/5. p 171
    To pay levy on 3 tytheables to Mr Ja Bagnall. 6 Feb 1654/5.
    p 174

Loes, Mr. Richard. of Lancaster, planter. Cattle and crop mortgaged
     to him by Tho Griffeth. 22 Nov 1654. p 182
          His a/c included in settlemt of Lawson est. 20 Jan 1655/6.p 192
          Justice. 6 June 1655. p 196
          Wit assignmt of land Johnson to Gregory. 14 Aug 1654. p 218
          To pay levy on 3 tytheables to Mr Bagnall. 7 Dec 1655. p 236
          Justice. 6 Jan 1655/6. p 244
Loyd, Mr. To pay levy on 2 tytheables to Mr Jno Catlet. 6 Feb 1654/5
     p 174
Longworth, Alice. Headright of Mr Jas Bagnall. 6 Aug 1655. p 208
Lodwell, Jere. Headright of Capt Hen Fleet. 24 Oct 1653. p 89
Lunce, Edw. Headright of Mr Tho Carter. 6 Feb 1654/5. p 172
Lunsford, Lady Elizabeth (entered on list as 'La Lunsford'). To pay
     levy on 12 tytheables to Mr Jno Cox. 6 Feb 1654/5. p 174
          To pay levy on 14 tytheables to Wm Leech. 7 Dec 1655. p 236
Lunte, David (this name open to question). See entry Mr Tho Hawkins.
     6 Aug 1655. p 209
Lusher, Elinor. Headright of Tho Lampkin. 6 Oct 1653. p 79
Lynell, Wm. He, with Hen Dedman, attaches the estate of Olis Segar.
     6 Apl 1654. p 140

Mackmum, Jas. Headright of Wm Tigner. 6 Apl 1653. p 43
Maddocke, Rice. A cow is owed him by Jno Robinson. 25 Oct 1655.p 213
Madestard, Thos Wit Rice Jones to Petterson. 22 Oct 1652. p 39
          Wit Seamor to Carter. 16 Mar 1652/3. p 47
          Wit Meredith to Marsh. 1 Apl 1654. p 134
          Wit Hackett to Nicholls. 24 Jan 1653/4. p 165
          Wit Griffith to Loes. 22 Nov 1654. p 182
          Wit Best to Williams and Porteus. 5 Feb 1654/5. p 184
          Wit Sharp to Brent. 11 Dec 1654. p 187
          Wit Clapham Jr to Steephenson. 12 July 1654. p 188
Malford, Tho. Headright of Capt More Fantleroy. 10 Jan 1652/3. p 27
Mallos Marga. Headright of Wm Clapham Jr. 6 June 1654. p 145
Mallory, Phillip, Clerk. Guardian of Tho Oldis vs Capt Tho Streator
     who married the relict of Col Tho Burbage decd, etc. To the
     Sheriffs of Nansemun, Elizabeth City, Northumberland and Lan-
     caster Counties. 17 March 1657/8. Northumberland Co Records,
     Vol.15. p 4
Maloy, Margarett. Was serv't to Epa Lawson decd. To serve 1/2 year.
     2 June 1652. p 10
Man, Sams To pay levy on 4 tytheables to Abra Weekes. 7 Dec 1655.
     p 237
Mannah, Tho. His base born child by Elizas Tomlin, by the will of
     the mother, to be kept by Roger Haris and his wife till 18. To
     be taught to read, write, etc. Haris to have all the tobo from
     Jno Robinson. etc. 6 June 1655. p 198
Mannaugh, Tho. See entry Eliz Tomlyn. 6 Feb 1653/4. p 138
Mannyng, Tho. Wit Ecevns to Lylly. 7 Mar 1652/3. p 36
Marks, Jno. Headright of Jno Weir. 6 Oct 1654. p 162

Markets. 6 June 1655. p 201. Places appointed for Stores and Markets:
"from Grimes Cove to the uper side of Tho Hopkins plantacon and
Tewsdaye to be the marked daye   N side"
"From Mr Rich: Perrots Creeke two myles Downwards and begininge
at Mr Fra: Coales Plantacon and wedensday to be the marked daye
S. side"
"from Mr Jas Bagnalls two myles upwards including his plantacon
Thursdaye to be the marked daye"
"from the uper side of Mr Gilsons Creeke two myles upwards
includeinge his plantacon Frydaye to be the marked daye"

Markets. Places appointed. This entry illegible. The name William
Clapham Jr appears. 25 Oct 1655. p 214

Markets. See entry Court House. 7 Dec 1655. p 233

Marsh, Mr. To pay levy on 4 tytheables to Maj: Jo: Carter. 7th Dec
1655. p 234

Marshall, Mary. Headright of V Stanford. 6 June 1655. p 198

Marshall, Roger. Wit trust transaction Chicheley for Wormeley. 18th
April 1654. p 129

Marshe, the widow. Her land adj that sold by Rd Bennett to Rd Loes.
4 June 1652. p 46

Marsh, Fra: deceased. His estate owes Jno Meade 3303 lb tobo, the
debt being assigned to Mr Wm Haier. 1200 lb being pd, order
that Tho Griffeth,who married the relict and extrx of Marsh,
pay Wm Clapham Jr, atty of Haier, the balance from the estate.
7 Aug 1654. p 151

Marsh, Geo. merchant. Buys 560 acres from Jno Meredith shipwright
on W side St Johns Creek. 1 Apl 1654. p 134
Wit: bond Carter to Carter. 1 June 1654. p 135

Marsh, Mrs Luc'e. Judgt agst her 250 lb tobo to Antho Jackman. 6th
April 1653. p 44

Martland, Michaell. See entry Maj: Jno Carter. 6 Oct 1653. p 79

Mascall, Robt. He was assigned 320 acres on N side Rappa by Richd
Coleman. No date shown. Mascall assigns his right in this land
to Rice Jones. 28 Feb 1652/3. pp 54-5

Mascall, Robt. Assignee of Domino Theriot. Impleads Wm Clapham Jr
for a debt of 3400 lb tobo due from estate of Epa Lawson dec'd,
and certain specialties in Clapham's hands. Clapham is ordered
to deliver to Mascall a specialty of James Linche due the est.
and when Major Jno Carter's debt is pd "in whose behalfe the
said Clapham had Commission of Administracon", the balance of
the debt due Mascall to be pd him. 6 Aug 1653. p 62

Mascall, Robt. Ordered to pay damages to Edw Grimes and Wm White
who he had "Causelesly" arrested. 8 Aug 1653. p 63

Mascall, Robt. "8ber 18th Richard Coleman hath ordered a Caveat for
an Administracon of his brother in Law Robt Mascalls Estate".
18 Oct 1653. p 80

Mascall, Robt. Deceased. His exor Wm Newsom ordered to pay Capt Hen
Fleet 420 lb tobo. 9 Dec 1653. p 100

Mashcaell, Jno. Headright of Mr Row Lawson. 6 Feb 1654/5. p 172

Maxy, Jno. Headright of Mr Tho Carter. 6 Feb 1654/5. p 172

Maydstone, Tho. Was servant to Epaph: Lawson dec'd. To serve 2 yrs.
2 June 1652. p 10

Meader, Tho. Wit receipt Woodward to Williamson. 4 Dec 1653. p 87
See entry Lambert Lambertson. 31 Jan 1653/4. p 136
Appointed Constable. Mr Ja Williamson to admr oath. 6 Apl 1654.
p 141

Meader, Am'br. To appraise est of Tho Meads decd. 6 June 1655. p 197

Meads, Tho. Buys 700 acres, above Mr Jas Williamson's land, from Wm
Underwood. 12 Sept 1653. p 111

Meade, Jno. See entry Fra: Marsh, decd. 7 Aug 1654. p 151

Meads, Tho. His servt Bour Harison to serve extra time for running
away. 7 Aug 1654. p 152

Mead, Tho: To pay levy on 3 tytheables to Mr Ja Williamson. 6 Feb
1654/5. p 174

Mead, Mr. His a/c incl,in settlemt of Lawson est. 20 Jan 1655/6.
p 192

Meads, Tho. Deceased. Prob of his will to Geo Bryer. 6 June 1655.
p 197

Meades, Tho. A Court held at his house. 7 March 1655/6. p 209

Mead, Tho. Orphan. Petitions the Court that he may choose a guardian,
he being of sufficient age. Order that according to his desire,
he remain in guardianship of Mr Wm Underwood. 6 Aug 1655.p 209

Meade, Tho: of Rappa sells Miner Doeders 2 cows. Wit: Willi Underwood. Will Moesley. 17 Nov 1653. Recorded 1 Nov 1655. p 221

Meades, Tho. The son of Tho Meads dec'd. Mr Wm Underwood appointed
his guardian. His whole estate now in the hands of Geo Bries
to be delivered to Underwood. 7 Dec 1655. p 233

Mealey, Marga: Punished for having a base born child by Da: Grisley.
he to pay 1200 lb tobo to the parish. Mr Row Law: security.(Mr
Rowland Lawson). 6 Feb 1653/4. p 138

Meather, Tho. To pay levy on 2 tytheables to Mr Wm Underwood. 7 Dec
1655. p 234

Meder, Amb: To pay levy on 4 tytheables to Mr Toby Smyth. 24 Octr
1653. p 92

Merall, Geo. Headright of Toby Smith. 6 Oct 1652. p 16

Merick, Wm. Headright of Rd Perrott. 10 Jan 1652/3. p 26

Merideth, John. In dif with Wm Clapham Sr regarding the building of
a sloop, a shallop, etc. 10 Jan 1652/3. p 25
Wit: receipt Potter to Grimes. 30 Nov 1653. p 117
Patents 560 acres on West side toward the head of St Johns
Creek, etc. on 10 Oct 1652. John Meredith, shipwright, assigns
this land to Geo Marsh, merchant. Wit Tho Madestard. William
Hutchins. 1 Apl 1654. p 134
In regard to Edmonds estate see entry Edwin Conway. 6 Apl 1654.
p 140
As son in law of Mrs Frances Edmonds decd is appointed admr of
her est. 7 March 1653/4. p 142
See entry Elias Edmonds, deceased. 6 June 1654. p 144
As admr of Elias Edmonds obtains judgt agst Mr Jno Edward for
1835 lb tobo. 6 June 1654. p 145

Meredith, John. Appears as admr of Elias Edmonds decd. 7 Aug 1654.
    p 151
    Appears as admr, with Walter Herd, of Elias Edmonds decd. 7th
    Aug 1654. p 151
    Denies debt of 992 lb tobo when sued by Laws Phillips. 7 Aug
    1654. p 152
    To pay levy on 5 tytheables to Mr Clapham Sr. 6 Feb 1654/5.
    p 174
    Ref to as joint admr with Walter Herd of est of Elyas Edmonds.
    6 June 1655. p 199
    To have "quitus est" of est of Elias Edmonds. 25 Oct 1655. p 211
    To have use of the cattle for bringing up the children of Elias
    Edmonds. 25 Oct 1655. p 211
    Assignmt of 300 acres on NE side Corotomen river to him by
    Walter and Eliz Herd. 16 May 1655. p 227
    Assignmt of Herd's patent to him with grant of her part to Eliz
    Greene. 7 Dec 1655. p 231
    His bill 450 lb tobo to be delivered by Vincent Stanford to Mr
    Tho Bushrode. 7 Dec 1655. p 231
    To pay levy to V Stanford. 7 Dec 1655. p 235
    Buys land from Major Jno Bond. See entry his name. 4 Dec 1655.
    p 241
    Appears also as John Merryday. See Va Colonial Abstracts, Vol.
    20. p 8 for items concerning his marriages.
Meriman, John. List of cattle in his custody belonging to his
    children: 1 heifer given by Thomas Harwood to Eliz dau of
    Jno Meriman. 1 calf given by Mr Wm Neesom to Wm son of Jno
    Meriman. Recorded 7 Aug 1652. p 8
Meriman, Jno. Petitions for debt due him as attorney of Jno Cornelis
    of 1095 lb tobo from est of Epa Lawson decd. 10 Jan 1652/3. p 24
Meriman, Jno. A month's work of an able hand due him. See entry Jno
    Sharpe. 6 Apl 1653. p 44
    Assigned a serv't named John Snooke by Col Tho Burbage. 7 Mar
    1652/3. p 46
    To pay levy on 3 tytheables to Mr Tho Brice. 24 Oct 1653. p 91
    His land on a branch of Iland Neck Creek called Grymes Creek,
    etc. 14 Nov 1649. p 119
    See entry Major Jno Carter. 6 June 1654. p 145
    See entry Edw Boswell. 6 June 1654. p 146
    To pay levy on 2 tytheables to Mr Tho Brice. 6 Feb 1654/5. p 174
Meriman, John. He and Morgan Haynes patent - hundred acres adj John
    Paine on 26 Feb 1653/4. Jno Meriman and his wife Andred or
    Andrie Meriman assign all interest in the patent. Wit Thomas
    Coggan. Luke Davies. 9 Sept 1654. p 183
Merryman, Mr. To pay levy on 3 tytheables to Wm Neesham. 7 Dec 1655.
    p 237
Merrid, Jno. Ordered to pay 237 lb tobo to Jo Gundry. 25 Oct 1655.
    p 212
Meriwether, Nicho: Patents 400 acres on S side Rappa abt 6 miles
    up. Adj land of Dale, of Jas Bonner. 10 Feb 1653/4. He sells
    it to Hump Hagett. Wit: Anthoine Armell. Tho Humphrey. 3 Oct
    1654. Hagett sells it to Cuth Potter. Wit Rich Cole. 30 Oct
    1654. pp 178-9

Miles, David. To receive 20 stripes for threatening to strike his
    master, Mr John Carter, with his hoe. 25 Oct 1655. p 213
Millesent, Jno. Wit deed Hackett to Nicholls. 24 Jan 1653/4. p 165
    Wit mortgage Griffeth to Loes. 22 Nov 1654. p 182
Mills, Jno. To pay levy on 1 tytheable to Mr And Gilson. 6 Febry
    1654/5. p 174
Minor - See entry Miner Doerders who buys 2 cows from Tho Meade. 17
    Nov 1653. p 221
Mitchell, Thos. Wit P of A Kempe to Clarke. 9 Sept 1651. p 57
Mondegust, Cornelis. Wit P of A Montfort to Moseley. 12 Aug 1650.
    (date doubtful). p 83
Montford, Henry. Power of Attorney. Plainly dated 12 August 1659
    and just as plainly an error in copying by John Phillips the
    Clerk of Lancaster County. He records it 8 Oct 1653. The date
    is doubtless 1650 with a tail drawn down on the '0'.
    Peeter Pope, alias Depaus, notary pub., sworn by the Court of
    Holland and dwelling in the Citty of Roterdam. That Mr Henry
    Mountford of Roterdam, merchant, appoints his "well beloved
    friend" Mr Wm Moosle, merchant, in the Virginias to receive
    from Wm Underwood now dwelling in the Virginias, settlement of
    accounts, etc. Signed Henry Montford. Wit: Jeremias boucheret.
    Cornelis Mondegust. p. 83
    Receipt. Wm Mosele to Mr Wm Underwood for payment of all debts
    due Mr Henry Montfort, merchant in Roterdam. Witness: Will
    Moseley Junr. Dated 15 Jan 1650/1. Recorded 8 Oct 1653. p 84
    Also:
    Power of Attorney. 12 August 1650. Peter Pope alias Depaus,
    notary public in Roterdam, Holland. That John Shepheard of
    Roterdam, merchant, appoints "his welbeloved brother Wm Harris"
    to receive a/cs from Wm Underwood or James Williamson, merchts
    living in the Virginias, particularly for all goods delivered
    "the sd Williams" in the absence of Underwood by Jas Croscombe
    "in the late end of the year 1648", etc. Signed John Shepheard.
    Wit: Jeremias boucherot. Abraham Shepheard. Recorded in Lanc.
    Co. 8 Oct 1653. pp 84-5
    Also:
    Power of Atty. 14 Jan 1650/1. Will Harris to "beloved friend"
    Jas Astell to collect a/c for John Shepheard. Wit: John Byram.
    Charles Hill. Michael Top. Wm Thomas. pp 85-6
    Also:
    Receipt. 1 Feb 1650/1. Jas Astell to Mr Wm Underwood for paymt
    of a/c due John Shepheard merchant of Roterdam. Wit Wm Moseley.
    Hen. Huberd. Recorded 8 Oct 1653. p 86

Moone, Abraham. Security for Jno Phillips when appointed Clerk and
    Sheriff of Lancaster Co. 1 July 1652. p 1
    Nonsuited in dif with Wm Wratton. 10 Jan 1652/3. p 24
    Dif betw him and Domino Theriott to next Court. 10 Jan 1652/3.
    p 26

Moone, Abraham. Assignee of Jno Hollis. A suit long depending betw
    him and Domino Theriett admr of Henry Lee decd, for a debt of
    2000 lb tobo. Moone given liberty to settle at next Court. 6th
    Aug 1653. p 61
    See entry Jno Carter. 6 Oct 1653. p 79
    To pay levy on 14 tytheables to Mr Jno Cox. 24 Oct 1653. p 93
    He gives James Allison (or Aklison) a calf now at plantation
    of Sir Hen: Chisley in Rappa River. Wit: Wm Leech. Philip Bend-
    ridge. 18 Oct 1653. Recorded 10 Jan 1653/4. p 103
    Grant from Sir Wm Berkeley, 500 acres adj land of Jno Lilley
    on S side of Mulford Haven, land of Peeter Rigby, land of Jno
    Smyth, etc. 6 June 1650. p 106. He assigns this land to Tho
    Bourne. Wit: Edw Wiatt. Jno Jacksen. 26 May 1652. p 106
    Wit deed Pedro to Brocas. 13 Nov 1653. p 118
    Attorney for Col Rd Lee. 6 Feb 1653/4. p 138
    To survey land of Abra Weekes on petition of Da Wealch. 6 Feb
    1653/4. p 138
    Judgt agst him 600 lb tobo to Paul Brewer. 6 Apl 1654. p 140
    Complained agst by Edw Boswell. 6 June 1654. p 145
    Court order that Mr Bartram Hobert and Mr Willis view his crop
    and report damage. 7 Aug 1654. p 151
    Certificate for transporting 6 persons: 'An his wife', John
    Brewton, Wm Attawaye, Ja: Aklison, Eliza Paine, Jno Craford.
    7 August 1654. p 153
    Judgt to him agst est of Rd Lake decd for 600 lb tobo on testi-
    mony of Geo Waddinge. 6 Oct 1654. p 164
    Indented with Jno Edwards chirurgeon fer a hhd tobo for setting
    his dislocated shoulder and no cure effected. Edwards ordered
    to return the tobo. 6 Feb 1654/5. p 171
    Judgt for 1300 lb tobo agst est of Rd Lake decd to be pd by
    Geo Kibble admr. 6 Feb 1654/5. p 173
    In dif with Sir Henry Chichley. 6 Feb 1654/5. p 173
    As atty of Jno Jefferyes is in dif with Mr Edwin Conaway. Ref
    to next Court. 6 Feb 1654/5. p 173
    To pay levy on 7 tytheables to Mr Jno Cox. 6 Feb 1654/5. p 174
    Sold land to Arth: Dun. See entry his name. 6 June 1655. p 196
    Fails to appear when sued by Wm Copland. 6 June 1655. p 196
    His suit vs Tho Bourne to next Court. 6 June 1655. p 197
    Sues Arth: Dun. Does not appear. Is nonsuited. 6 June 1655.
    p 198
    His attorney Jno Phillips confesses judgt to Wm Coopland for
    2000 lb tobo at 1 yrs int. 6 Aug 1655. p 208
    Wit: Roughton to Brathatt. 27 Sept 1655. p 216 (Abra Moune)
Moraticon. See entry 'Muster'. 8 Aug 1653. p 65
Morill, David. Headright of Capt Hen Fleet. 24 Oct 1653. p 89
Moroughaw, Kath: Headright of Mr Toby Smith. 7 Aug 1654. p 151
Moroway a hylander. Headright of Capt More Fantleroy. 1 July 1652.
    p 1
Moseley, Mr. To pay levy on 2 tytheables to Mr Geo Taylor. 24 Oct
    1653. p 92
Moseley, Eliza. Headright of Rice Jones. 6 Aug 1652. p 2

Moseleye, Geo. His land adjs patent of Rich Colman on S side Rappa.
   14 Sept 1650. p 206
Moseley, Wm. See entry Hen: Montford. 12 Aug 1650. p 83
   Wit receipt Astell to Underwood. 1 Feb 1650/1. p 86
   Assigns interest in land to Elex Fleming. 6 Aug 1655. p 214
   Is assigned interest in land by Wm Underwood. 7th - 1652. p 214
   Wit deed Meade to Doerders. 17 Nov 1653. p 221
Moseley, Wm Jr. Wit receipt Wm Moseley to Wm Underwood. 8 Oct 1653.
   p 84
Moss, Robt. Dif betw him as pltf and Robt Tomlyn deft to next Court.
   6 Apl 1654. p 140
   To pay levy on 4 tytheables to Mr And Gilson. 6 Bebry 1654/5.
   p 174
   To pay levy on 3 tytheables to Mr Felson. 7 Dec 1655. p 238
Mottrom, Mr Jno. Formerly owned 600 acres on N side Peancketanok
   River. See entry Rd Lake. 5 Oct 1653. p 107
Mungoe, Jo: Wit deed Bond to Greene. Recorded 5 Jan 1655/6. p 242
Murren, Wm. Headright of Capt Hen Fleet. 6 June 1655. p 198

Muster. Orders dated 8 August 1653. p 65.
   On 21st day at 7'ber (September) next The Commissioners to
   meet at Mr Underwood's, etc., with XXX every 6th man raised
   in their limits.
   Mr Wm Underwood. Every 6th man sufficiently armed to meet at
   his house for a genl Randevous.
   Mr Coxes limits from Ja Benets upward to Mr Burnhams.
   Mr Rich: Loes from Parotts Creeke to Dedmans Creek.
   Mr Ja Bagnall from Dedmans Creek to the upper side of Puscati-
   oon and Mr Andrew Gilson from Puscaticon to the head of the
   river
   Mr Geo Taylors limits from the head of the river to Captt
   Fleets Plantation at Rappahannock
   Mr Wm Underwood from his own house to upper side of Totoskey
   Creeke to the upper side of Moraticom.
   Mr Da Fox from lower side of Moraticand to Mr Brices
   Mr Tho Brices limits from his own house to upper side of
   Corotowamon.
   And Major Jno Carter and Mr Row Lawson from Eastward side of
   Corotomen to the mouth of the river
                                        Teste   Jno Phillips

Mynshem, Eliza. Headright of And Gilson. 6 Oct 1654. p 162
Myrritt, Wm. Headright of Capt More Fantleroy. 10 Jan 1652/3. p 27

Narrow Neck. On W side Corotomen River. 1 Nov 1653. p 180
Nathan, Jno. Headright of Mr Ja Bagnall. 6 Aug 1655. p 208
Naylor, Tho. Headright of David Fox. 6 Oct 1652. p 15
Neale, Wm. Buys, with Jno Vauss, 600 acres on S side Rappa from Rich
   Colman. 4 June 1655. p 206

Needles, Jno. Wit deed Lake to Rigby. 5 Oct 1653. p 107

Nedles, Jno. To pay levy on 2 tytheables to Mr Tho Bourne. 6 Febry
    1654/5. p 174

Needles, Jno. To pay levy on 3 tytheables to Mr Kempe. 7 Dec 1655.
    p 239

Neesom, Mr Wm. Gave a calf to Wm son of Jno Meriman prior to 7 Aug
    1652. p 8

Neesham, Wm. Appraises est of Wm Foote decd. 10 Jan 1652/3. p 23

Newsome, Wm. His land on N side Rappa adjs that sold by Rice Jones
    to Howell Powell. 8 Jan 1652/3. p 51

Newsome, Wm. His land near patent of 320 acres to Rd Coleman. No
    date shown. Prior to 1653. pp 54-5

Newsam, Wm. Certificate for 250 acres in that his patent for 800
    acres was short that amount. 6 Aug 1653. p 61

Newsan, Wm. Given a heifer in partnership with Jno Pinn by Michaell
    Batersby. 21 Mar 1652/3. p 66

Newsam, Wm et als. Land grant to Wm Newsam, Thomas Sacks, Myles
    Batesby and John Pinn. 800 acres called Island Neck on N side
    Rappahannock near Corotomen, for transporting 16 persons. 29th
    Jan 1649/50. p 69.   Myles Battersby sells his interest in this
    land to Newsam and Pinn. Wit: Edwin Conaway. Howell Powell. 21
    March 1652/3. p 70.   Newsam and Pinn (here as Pine)
    assign their interests in this land to Tho Sacks. Wit: Edwin
    Conaway. Howell Powell. 22 March 1652/3. p 71.
    Also: Land Grant to Wm Newsam, Tho Sax, Myles Battersby and
    John Pinn, 550 acres on N side Rappa River in Northumberland
    Co. p 72.   Battersby assignes his interest in this 550 acres
    to Wm Newsam and Jno Pinn. 21 March 1652/3. p 73.
    Also: Tho Sax assigns his int in 800 acres to Wm Newsam and
    Jno Pine. 22 March 1642. Plainly this date in the original is
    an error and should be 1652/3. p 72

Newsam, Wm. To pay levy on 5 tytheables to Mr Tho Brice. 24th Oct
    1653. p 91

Newsam, Wm. As exor of Robt Mascall decd is ordered to pay Capt Hen
    Fleet 420 lb tobo. 9 Dec 1653. p 100

Newsam, Wm. Exor of Edw Grime. 1 Aug 1653. p 124

Neesham, Wm. Appraised est of Hen Lee. 7 Mar 1652/3. p 126

Neesam, Wm. Pd by Capt More Fantleroy a debt due from estate of Epa
    Lawson, decd. 6 June 1654. p 145

Neesam, Wm. See entry Edw Boswell. 6 June 1654. p 146

Neesham, Wm. Court order that he keep Ha- Harison until the next
    Court when Geo Beach is to appear and answer misdemeanors
    towards her and her brother. 6 June 1654. p 146

Neesham, Wm. To pay levy on 6 tytheables to Mr Tho Brice. 6th Feb
    1654/5. p 174

Neasham, Wm. "to take care for the Building of A Court house" on
    land formerly Downman's. His charge to be pd "by the Publique".
    25 Oct 1655. p 212

Neesom, Wm. To collect levies that were to be collected last year
    by Mr Thomas Bries. 7 Dec 1655. p 232

Neesham, Willm. To be pd 1979 of tobo from Co levy by Willm Leech
toward building the Court House. 7 Dec 1655. p 236
To receive levy for 54 tytheables from 17 persons, incl 7 for
himself. Also "To detaine in his owne hands towards the build-
ing of the Courthouse 2211 lb tobo. 7 Dec 1655. p 237
The next Court for lower part of the County, 6th Feb., at his
house if the Courthouse is not built. 7 Dec 1655. p 240
Nesam, Anth: late of this county, dec'd. Died without will. Admr to
Hen: Dedman as greatest creditor. 8 Dec 1653. p 96
Nethercotes, Nicho: Wit deed Pettibone to Cox. 1 Dec 1655. p 224
New Haven Creek. Abt 39 miles up on N side Rappa adj patent to Edw
James. 4 Jan 1653/4. p 184
Newman, Tho. Wit deed James to Best. 5 Sept 1654. p 184
Nickering, Nolas. Headright of Mr Row Lawson. 6 Feb 1654/5. p 172
Nickolls, Hen. Buys 150 acres from Evan Davis. See entry his name.
27 Mar 1653. p 50
Files mark for cattle and hogs. No date but of 10 Dec 1653.
p 133
Wit deed Lewis to Willis and Watkins. 7 Aug 1654. p 155
Patent. 29 July 1652. 200 acres on NW side SW branch of Sunder-
land Creek, opp land of Denis Coniers and Evan Davies, etc.Hen
Nicholls, planter, of Lancaster Co, assigns this land to Jno
Jonson. Wit: Row Burnham. Evan Davies. 25 Apl 1653. p 157
Nichalls, Jas. Name entered on list (Mr David Fox's list) for County
levy but number of tytheables not shown. The name is written
between those to be collected from and those to be paid with
no notation. 24 Oct 1653. p 91
Nicolls, James. To be pd 3 hhd tobo for wages by Raleigh Travers. 6
Feb 1654/5. p 172
Nichols, Ja: To pay levy on 1 tytheable to Da: Fox. 7 Dec 1655.p 238
Nicklis, Jno. The name also appears as Nickloas in the entry. A long
letter to him from Nickloas George. See entry his name. Refers
to "your cosen Taverner and his wife" in England. 30 Oct 1652.
p 36
Nicholls, Jno. To pay levy on 2 tytheables to Mr Row Lawson. 24th
Oct 1653. p 90
Nicholls, John of Corotomen river, Lancaster Co, planter, leases for
2 yrs, to Andrew Boyer of the same place, planter, 350 acres on
E side of NW branch of Rappa Corotomen river being a branch of
Rappa river. Adjs land of Mrs Goldsmith, the land of said John
Nicholls, the land of Nichollas George, etc. Wit: Edwin Conaway.
Martha Conaway. 22 Dec 1652. p 114
In agreemt with Geo Nicholas to div 700 lb tobo equally. 13th
June 1653. p 115
His daughter reliet of Wm Downman decd. 6 June 1654. p 145
To appraise est of Robt Perfect decd. 6 June 1654. p 146
Settles est of Wm Downman decd. 6 Oct 1654. p 164
Buys 400 acres on E side Corotomen. Adjs his own land, that of
Mr Conaway, that of Mr George, from Capt Tho Hackett. 24 Jan
1653/4. p 165

Nicholls, Jno. To pay levy on 1 tytheable to Mr Clapham Sr. 6 Feb
    1654/5. p 174
Nichols, Jo. To pay levy to V Stanford. Also to be pd by Mr Stanford
    "To Jo Nicholls his sonne to remaine in his hands for publique
    0531 lb tobo". 7 Dec 1655. p 235
Nicholls, Wm of Lanc Co, planter, mortgages a cow called Naughtie to
    Wm Linell of same Co, planter, for 1000 lb tobo. Wit: Alex
    Flamingo. Tho Carter. 30 Nov 1653. p 105
Nickson, Jane. Headright of Nich Feyman. 6 Feb 1653/4. p 139
Noble, Jno. Headright of Hugh Brent. 6 Feb 1654/5. p 171
North, Anth: Headright of Mr And Gilson. 6 Oct 1654. p 162
Nutmeg quarter. See entry Toby Smith. 29 Sept 1647. p 81-2
Nuttall, Robt. Headright of Capt More Fantleroy. 10 Jan 1652/3. p 27

Obert, Mr Bartram. His land on S side Rappa. See entry Capt William
    Brocas, 18 Nov 1653. p 133
    His land adj Rich Lewis on S side Rappa, near head of Nyemcook
    Creek. 29 Nov 1652. p 155
    To pay levy on 2 tytheables to Mr Rich Perrott. 6 Feb 1654/5.
    p 174
    To appraise the estate of Jo Johnson and his brothers and his
    sisters. Robt Burton their guardian. 7 Dec 1655. p 231
    To pay levy on 2 tytheables to Abra Weekes. (in this entry as
    "Mr Hoberts"). 7 Dec 1655. p 237
Obert see Hobart.
Obarts Creek. On S side Rappa. See entry Capt Wm Brocas. 18th Nov
    1653. p 133
Odam, Hen. Headright of Tho Paine. 6 Oct 1652. p 15
Oldis, Tho. See entry Rev Phillip Mallory. 17 March 1657/8/
Orenge, Thos. Headright of Wm Clapham Sr. 6 Oct 1652. p 15
Orley. See Fox family memo.
Othersone, Mary. Headright of Hugh Brent. 6 Feb 1654/5. p 171
Oudlantt, Cornelius. Wit Petterson to Baning. 29 Oct 1652. p 39

Page, Robt. Headright of Capt More Fantleroy. 10 Jan 1652/3. p 27
Paine, Mr. To pay levy on 5 tytheables to Mr Tho Brice. 24 Oct 1653.
    p 91
    To pay levy on 5 tytheables to Mr Jas Bagnall. 24 Oct 1653.
    p 94
    To be pd from levy "for provision for the Burgesses 0140 lb
    tobo". 24 Oct 1653. p 95
Paine, Eliza. Headright of Abra Moone. 7 Aug 1654. p 153
Paine, John. By testimony of Mrs Martha Brice and Mary Arundell
    proves that Ann Rixam has slandered his wife. The Rixam woman
    ordered to acknowledge her fault in Court and her husband,
    Xpoffer Rixam (Rixham), to pay charges. 6 Aug 1652. p 3
    Is pd 100 lb tobo from levy for his boat. 10 Jan 1652/3. p 29
    Wit: Powell to Sneade. 14 March 1652/3. p 52. See next entry.

Paine, Jno. Half of 300 acres bought by him and Tho Powell from Wm
    Clapham belongs to Charles Sneade, Paine having sold Sneade his
    share. 5 Dec 1652. p 48
    Buys land on creek called 'hapie Harbor' from Tho Brice. 25th
    July 1653. p 67
    To view work done by Jno Pedro for Mr Row Burnham and report
    to Court. 6 Oct 1653. p 77
    To be pd 1240 lb tobo from levy "for boat hire and press'con".
    24 Oct 1653. p 91
    To be pd from levy "for Boat hire for the burgesses 1100 lb
    tobo. 24 Oct 1653. p 95
    Security for Jno Pedro in debt of 400 lb tobo. 8 Dec 1653.p 96
    To 'vew' Mr Rawleigh Travers' tobacco house and report. 6 Feb
    1654/5. p 172
    To pay levy on 7 tytheables to Mr Tho Brice. 6 Feb 1654/5.p 174
    He and Margaret his wife assign int in a patent to Charles
    Snead. Wit: Humph Booth, Vinc Stanford. 21 Oct 1654. p 183
    Certificate for land for importing John Paine Jr, Mary Paine,
    Wm Emerson, Marie Wms, Eliza Pusie. 6 Aug 1655. p 209
    To receive levy on 35 tytheables incl 1 tytheable for himself.
    7 Dec 1655. p 239
Paine, Penelope. Headright of Tho Paine. 6 Oct 1652. p 15
Paine, Ralph. Sued by Capt More Fantleroy who did not appear. Case
    dismissed. 6 Oct 1652. p 17
    To be pd 100 lb tobo by Elyas Blake for loss of time in suit
    betw Blake and Jno Phillips. 9 Dec 1653. p 100
    Wit. P of A Tho Paine to Raleigh Travers. 6 Dec 1653. p 103
    Patent. 27 Oct 1652. 250 acres on S side Rappa up Coxes' Creek,
    etc.   He sells this land to Jno Killman, Geo Killman and Tho
    For- (possibly Forest). Wit: Jno Weir. Rich Hall. 6 Oct 1654.
    Recorded 10 Oct 1654. p 160
Paine, Tho. Certificate 150 acres for importing Hen: Odam. Penelope
    Paine. Joane Staples. 6 Oct 1652. p 15
    Pd 100 lb tobo from levy for a wolf. 10 Jan 1652/3. p 29
    Dif betw him and Hen Dodman re land to next Court. Capt More
    Fantleroy, Mr Toby Smith and Mr Tho Brice to report on bound-
    ries. 6 Oct 1653. p 78
    Order that he be pd debt of 6 bbl corn by Capt More Fantleroy.
    9 Dec 1653. p 100
    Dif betw him and Capt Fantleroy to next Court. Paine to pro-
    duce certain specialties of Fantleroy's in hands of Mr Wethall,
    etc. 9 Dec 1653. p 100
    P of A to Mr Raleigh Travers to implead Capt Fantleroy. Wit.
    Clem't Thrush. Ralph Paine. 6 Dec 1653. p 103
    To appraise est of Tho Steephens dec'd. 7 Aug 1654. p 153
    To pay levy on 6 tytheables to Mr Ja Bagnall. 6 Feb 1654/5.
    p 174
    To pay levy on 4 tytheables to Mr Smith. 7 Dec 1655. p 239
Parishes. Lancaster County divided into 2 parishes. Boundries
    refer to land of Richard Bennot, Esqr., now in possession of
    Rice Jones, etc. 7 Aug 1654. p 152

Parker, Tho. Wit receipt Whettell to Wmson. 11 May 1651. p 6

Parmiter, Jo. To pay levy on 1 tytheable to Mr Lucas. 7 Dec 1655.
p 238

Parrey, Ral: Headright of Mr Tho Hawkins. 6 Aug 1655. p 208

Parrey, Robt. Headright of Rice Jones. 6 Aug 1652. p 2

Parr, Robt. Wit receipt Perott to Allen. See Allen entry. 23rd Oct
1649. p 48

Parsons, Sarah. Wit Smith-Fantleroy of Nansemum transaction. See
entry Toby Smith. 29 Sept 1647. pp 81-2

Patteson, Mr. To pay levy on 2 tytheables to Abra Weekes. 7th Dec.
1655. p 237

Pattison, Tho. Assigned land by Tho Keds. 8 Oct 1655. p 219
Entry shows him as of Lanc. Co. He, with Richd Bridges, buys
200 acres from Thos Keds. 16 Apl 1655. p 219

Pedro, John. He and Evan Davis sell a neck of land to Richd White
and John Wealch (also as Welch in the entry). Adjs land of
Denis Coniers and Evan Davis. Wit: Edw Boswell. Richd: Cole.
23 May 1652. p 45
Dif betw him and Mr Row Burnham to next Court. 6 Oct 1653.p 77
Ordered to pay Mr Row: Burnham 400 lb tobo for failing to meet
agreemt concerning building. John Paine and Nich: Ferman go his
security. 8 Dec 1653. p 96
He, with Evan Davies, buys land on Sunderland Creek from Edwd
Boswell 16 May 1653. Davies assigns his interest to Pedro who
sells the whole property to Capt Wm Brocas Esqr 13 Nov 1653.
p 118
His land on S side Rappa: See entry Capt Wm Brocas. 18 Nov 1653.
p 133

Peirce, Mary. Headright of David Fox. 6 Oct 1652. p 15

Pepeticke Creek. See Tho Lucas. 7 June 1652. p 221

Perfect, Robt. Gives his son Tho Perfect a cow. His dau Frances is
given a heifer by Tho Powell. 19 Jan 1652/3. p 22. (Note: How
would you like to live up to that name ? As sweet and pure as
I am, I'd hate to attempt it. I attempt to be accurate, but the
name is there just the same. Not forgetting an old friend of
mine, an old rip of a Madam, who apologised for herself in
remarking 'Nobody is PERFECT, and nobody ever has been'. B.F.)
Since this is a volume of history here is Note No. 2. The
female referred to was no less than the all too well known
buxom and blondined Miss Annie Bowman. B.F.

Perfect, Robt. Several differences betw him and Elyas Edmonds to
next Court. 6 Oct 1653. p 77. (Here is evidence that our
smart ancestors did not even know what was perfect. B.F.

Perfect, Robt. Deceased. (We are now done with perfection. The lady
hastens from her exalted state to become a mere queen). Admr
of his estate to Charles Kinge who married the relict. Thos
Powell security. Thos Powell and Jno Nicholls to appraise the
estate. 6 June 1654. p 146

Perrot, Mr. Richd. Or however you care to spell his name. The
differences in these early records are sufficient to please
all tastes. See next page.

Perrott, Mr. Richard. Com of admr of est of Hen Dedman decd to him.
6 June 1655. p 196
A Court held at his house last June. 7 Dec 1655. p 233
"Mr Parretts upper plantacon" to pay levy on 2 tytheables to
Mr Bagnall. 7 Dec. 1655. p 236
To pay levy on 6 tytheables to Abra Weekes. 7 Dec 1655. p 237
(The foregoing entries were all in the name of 'Mr Perrott'.
Perrott, Richard. Certificate for importing 6 persons. 10 Jan 1652/3.
p 26
Nonsuited in action vs Wm Jonson. 10 Jan 1652/3. p 27
The servant he bought from Mr Grigs agreed that wages due from
Wm Johnson now to be due to Perrott. Signed Sa: Gooch. Sworn
before Toby Smith and David Fox. 24 Feb 1652/3. p 45
He and Sara his wife. See involved relationships shown in entry
under Charles Allen. 23 Oct 1649. p 48
Certificate for land for importing Sarah Keys, Da: Simpson, Wm
Dunston and Hen Sharpe. 6 Oct 1653. p 77
To collect levy on 36 tytheables from 10 persons incl 4 for
himself. 24 Oct 1653. p 93
To collect levy on 57 tytheables incl 5 tytheables of his own.
6 Feb 1654/5. p 174
To appraise est of Capt Wm Brocas decd. 7 May 1655. p 189
Appears as a Justice at a Court held at his house. 6 June 1655.
p 196
Justice. 6 Aug 1655. p 207 (here as 'Mr Rich Parrett')
Justice. 25 Oct 1655. p 210
P of A from Tho Lucas to deliver 600 acres to Tho Hawkins. 3rd
Feb 1654/5. p 218 (here as 'Mr Richerds Parratt')
Parotts Creek. See entry 'Muster'. 8 Aug 1653. p 65
See entry 'Markets'. 6 June 1655. p 201
Peirse, Will. Wit P of A Lucas to Parratt. 3 Feb 1654/5. p 218
Perry, Mr. To pay levy on 2 tytheables to Mr Bagnall. 7 Dec 1655.
p 236
Perry, Saml. Ordered to pay 2700 lb tobo to Geo Collins in a long
tedious suit. 7 Dec 1655. p 231
Peeters, Hen: Headright of Jo: Eyers. 6 Aug 1655. p 208
Peeters, Alice. Headright of Fra: Gower. 24 Oct 1653. p 89
Pettit, Mr. To pay levy on 1 tytheable to Mr Felson. 7 Dec 1655.
p 238
Peterson, Elnor. (here as 'Peeterson') Headright of Jno Gillet. 6th
Oct 1654. p 162
Peeterson, Ever. Headright of Epe Boney. 10 Jan 1652/3. p 26
Petterson, Evan. Buys 350 acres, known as Muskeeto Poynt, from Rice
Jones 22 Oct 1652. Sells it, through his atty Walter Bruce, to
Ebber Baning. 29 Oct 1652. p 39 (The Evers and Ebbers have
been long forgotten - but the Muskeetoes are right there right
now. Don't forget that.)
Pettibone, Richd. Assigns to Jno Cox of London, haberdasher, all int
in 700 acres on S side Rappa. Wit: Nicholas Nethercots. 6th
March 1648/9. p 223. Recorded 25 Nov 1655.

Pettibone, Richard. Patent. 700 acres on S side Rappa. Boundries illegible. 23 Nov 1648. p 223

Pettibone, Richard of the County of Nanzemum in Virginia, planter, sells 700 acres in Rappa River on S side, patent dated 23 Nov 1648, to Jno Cox of London, haberdasher, and now resident in Virginia. Signed Richard Pettibone. Wit: Nicholas Nethercotes, Robert Lewis. 6 March 1648/9. Recorded 1 Dec 1655. p 224

Phelps see Felps.

Phelps, David. Nonsuit to him, he having been arrested at suit of Tho Breamer who did not appear. 7 Dec 1655. p 232

Philipps, Mr. To pay levy on 3 tytheables to Mr Da: Fox. 7 Dec 1655. p 238

Philips, John. Appointed Clerk and Sheriff. Abra Moone security. 1st July 1652. p 1

Wit deed Jackman to Edgecomb. 29 Dec 1652. p 19

Is pd 400 lb from Co levy. 10 Jan 1652/3. p 29

Sheriff of Lancaster Co. 6 Jan 1652/3. p 32

Wit: recording of letter George to Nicklis. 8 Jan 1652/3. p 36

Judgt agt him to Wm Clapham Jr for amt due from Tho Ro—. 6 Apl 1653. p 44

A Court held at his house. 6 Aug 1653. p 61

As Clerk. See 'Muster'. 8 Aug 1653. p 65

Wit deed Brice to Paine. 25 July 1653. p 67

Judgt to Wm Clapham Senr agst him, 660 lb tobo, if Tho Roots fails to appear at next Court. 6 Oct 1653. p 79

To pay levy on 2 tytheables to Mr Da Fox. 24 Oct 1653. p 91

He and his wife Sarah involved in slander suit. See entry Mrs Joane Thomas. 9 Dec 1653. p 99

Was sued by Elyas Blake. 9 Dec 1653. p 100

Wit deed Underwood to Meads. 12 Sept 1653. p 111

Wit will Edw Grime. 1 Aug 1653. p 124

Wit deed Smyth to Webb. 6 Feb 1653/4. p 128

Judgt agt him for L 19. 16. 0 Sterling for nonappearance of Mr Conaway at suit of Jno Jeffrys. 6 Apl 1654. p 141

Dif betw him and Wm Thomas to next Court. 6 Oct 1654. p 164

Wit deed Taylor to Tomlyn. 6 Oct 1654. p 166

To pay levy on 3 tytheables to Mr Da: Fox. 6 Feb 1654/5. p 174

To "make a sirvey". See entry Arth: Dun. 6 June 1655. p 196

Sued by Wm Copland 1000 lb tobo for nonappearance of Abraham Moone. 6 June 1655. p 196

Sued by Wm Clapham Jr, atty of Jas Hannum, for nonappearance of Tobyas Horton. 6 June 1655. p 196

Confesses judgt, on behalf of Abra Moone, to Wm Coopland for 2ooo lb tobo at 1 yrs interest. 6 Aug 1655. p 208.

Appears as Sheriff of Lancaster Co. 25 Oct 1655. p 212

Deceased. The 500 lb tobo to be pd him from last year's levy for procuring Acts of Assembly, to be pd to Mr Edw Dale, now Clerk of the Court, for obtaining the Acts. 7 Dec 1655. p 240

Phillips, Law: Sues Jno Meredith for debt of 992 lb tobo. Meredith denies the debt. 7 Aug 1654. p 152

Pig, John. Wit deed of gift Chicheley to Conway. 7 May 1653. p 68

Piksbury, Cha: Headright of Mr Ja Bagnall. 6 Aug 1655. p 208

Pine see Pinn.

Pine, Jno. Buys land, with Will Keegam, from Edw Lilly. 7 Sept 1652.
   p 40

Pinn, Jno. Is given a heifer in partnership with Wm Newsan. 21 Mar
   1652/3. p 66
   See entry Wm Newsam et als. 29 Jan 1649/50. p 69

Pitt, Robt. 400 lb tobo to have been pd him by Mr Eap Lawson deed
   for the use of Wm Jonson. 6 June 1655. p 201

Place, Fran: To pay levy on 1 tytheable to Jno Paine. 7 Dec 1655.
   p 239

Playce, Rich. Headright of Capt More Fantleroy. 10 Jan 1652/3.p 27

Playce, Tho. Headright of Capt More Fantleroy. 10 Jan 1652/3. p 27

Plummer, Wm. Wit Sharpe to Dudley et als. 6 Feb 1651/2. p 119

Pope, Peeter. Notary Public of the City of Roterdam, etc. See entry
   Hy Montford. 12 Aug 1650. p 83

Poplar Neck. Owned by Tho Brice. Adj a creek called "hapie Harbor".
   25 July 1653. p 67

Porter, Kath: Headright of Capt Wm Brocas. 6 Oct 1652. p 16

Portus, Alexander. (Porteus). Certificate for land for his own
   transportation and that of Eliza: Browne. 7 Aug 1654. p 151

Porteus, Alexr. With Tho Wms buys 350 acres from Tho Best. 5 Feby
   1654/5. p 184

Potter, Cuthbert. Headright of Sir Henry Chisley. 10 Jan 1652/3. In
   this entry as 'Cuthberd Potter'. p 27
   Wit deed of gift Chicheley to Conway. 7 May 1653. p 68
   Wit receipt Conway to Brocas. 15 May 1653. p 69
   Letter from Daniell Howes to appear at Court for him. 26 May
   1653. p 87
   P of A from Jno Custise of Northampton Co, merchant, to receive
   a/cs due from admrs of Jno Eaton, merchants dec'd. 26th July
   1653. p 88
   Atty of Jno Custice. See entry Jno Eaton. 8 Dec 1653. p 97
   As atty of Capt Daniell How, sues Wm White for debt of 958 lb
   tobo. Also sues Wm Wrahton (Wm Wraughton) for 303 lb tobo. 8th
   Dec 1653. p 97
   As atty of Capt Daniell Howe, acquits Marga'tt Grimes widow of
   Edwd Grimes of a bill for 800 lb tobo passed by her husband to
   Mr Fox and assigned by him to Howe. Wit Jno Meredith. Edwin
   Conaway. 30 Nov 1653. p 117
   Wit deed Pedro to Brocas. 13 Nov 1653. p 118
   Wit assignmt Chicheley to Brocas. 6 Feb 1653/4. p 133
   As atty of Capt Da: Howe to be pd 303 lb tobo by Wm Wraughton.
   6 Feb 1653/4. p 137
   Buys 400 acres, on S side Rappa abt 6 miles up, from Humph
   Hagett. 30 Oct 1654. p 178
   Wit Welch to Coopland. 6 June 1655. p 194

Powell, Mr. To pay levy on 3 tytheables to Mr Da Fox. 24 Oct 1653.
   p 91
   To pay levy on 7 tytheables to Mr Da: Fox. 6 Feb 1654/5. p 174

Powell, Mr. To pay levy on 6 tytheables to Da: Fox. 7 Dec 1655.p 238
Powell, Ben. Buys, in partnership with Edwd Dudley and Wm Downman,
   300 acres in Grymes Creek, from Jno Sharpe. 6 Feb 1651/2. p 119
   He sells 100 acres, part of 300 acres in Curotomen River in
   Rappa called Harwoods Neck. Wit. Jno Sharpe. Edw Grimes. 19th
   Nov 1652. p 216
Powell, Hopkin. Is pd 1123 lb tobo from Co levy. 10 Jan 1652/3. p 29
Powell, Howell. Wit deed Fantleroy to Roots. 8 July 1652. p 7
   Buys 408 acres from Rice Jones. See entry his name. 8th Jan
   1652/3. p 51
   He assigns 1/2 of 408 acres to Geo Haris. See entry Charles
   Sneade. Wit. Rice Jones. Geo Sleight. 12 Jan 1652/3. p 52
   He assigns 1/2 of 408 acres to Charles Sneade. Wit. Geo Beach.
   John Paine. 14 March 1652/3. Recorded 6 Apl 1653. p 52
   He is assigned 88 acres on N side Rappa by Rice Jones. 22 Jan
   1652/3. p 53
   He and Geo Haris are assigned 320 acres by Rice Jones. 28 Feb
   1652/3. pp 54-5
   He assigns his interest in 320 acres to Charles Sneade. 5 Mar
   1652/3. pp 54-5
   Wit deed of gift Batersby to Newsan and Pinn. 21 Mar 1652/3.
   p 66. Also see Newsam et als. 21 Mar 1652/3. p 70
   See entry Tho Powell. 19 Oct 1655. p 217
   Wit deed of Tho Hackett. 25 Oct 1655. p 226
   Wit Bond to Greene. Recorded 5 Jan 1655/6. p 242
Powell, Ri. Headright of Mr Ja Bagnell. 6 Aug 1655. p 208
Powell, Tho. Gives a heifer to Frances the dau of Robt Perfect. 19
   Jan 1652/3. p 22
   Acknowledges that 1/2 of a patent of 300 acres bought by him
   and John Paine from Wm Clapham belongs to Charles Sneade,Paine
   having sold Sneade his part. Wit. John Weir. Antho Fulgam. 5th
   Dec 1652. p 48
   To pay levy on 2 tytheables to Mr Tho Brice. 24 Oct 1653. p 91
   To appraise est of Robt Perfect decd. Also security for Charles
   Kinge the admr. 6 June 1654. p 146
   Headright of Jno Gillet. 6 Oct 1654. p 162
   To pay levy on 2 tytheables to Mr Tho Brice. 6 Feb 1654/5.
   p 174
   He and Howell Powell, planters, sell to Walter Herd 400 acres
   on upper W side Corotomen River, adj a creek div the land from
   Tho Hackett, etc. Wit. Howgh Lensey. Paull Kinsey. 19 Oct 1655.
   Recorded 1 Dec 1655. p 217
   Is in possession of land belonging to Wm Clapham on Corotomen
   River. 25 Oct 1655. p 226
   P of A from Walter and Eliz Herd. 25 Oct 1655. p 227
   To pay levy on 2 tytheables to Wm Neesham. 7 Dec 1655. p 237
Powell, Wm. Wit deed Downman to Kinge. 30 Sept 1652. p 120
Powling, Sebastian. Judgt to him for 143 lb tobo, bal of a/c for
   his wages from "the sd Mr Smyth". 24 Oct 1653. p 89. See next
   entry.

Powlinge, Sebastian. Arrested at suit of Mr Toby Smith in debt of
593 lb tobo. Failing to appear judgmt agst Jno Phillips the
Sheriff for this amt. 6 Oct 1654. p 163

Prettyman see Prittyman.

Price, Wm. Dif betw him and Jno Sherlock to next Court. 6 Feb 1654/5.
p 173
Has arrested Tho Walker for debt of 600 lb tobo which he trust-
ed him to receive of Humphrey Lee. That Walker, a non resident
of this County appeareth not but sent an account, etc, John
Sherlock his security. 6 June 1655. p 200

Pritchard, John, Gives "unto An my wife a crumple horned cow" to her
and the children born on her body forever. Recorded 6 Aug 1653.
p 58. (Note: I do hope this is not just a legal way of putting
off the milking on this unfortunate woman and the children. BF)

Pritchard, Jno. Fined 1000 lb tobo and disabled from taking oaths
in this Court. For "this day in open Court offer to depose unto
such things as were proved to be manifestly false". 24th Oct
1653. p 89

Pritchard, Jno. To pay levy on 1 tytheable to Mr Da Fox. 24 Oct 1653.
p 91
Judgt agst his cattle for debt of 565 lb tobo to Mr Tho Griffon.
9 Dec 1653. p 99

Prittiman, Mr Tho. Headright of Mr Toby Smith. 6 Aug 1655. p 209

Purifye, Tho. Sues Lambert Lambertson for 4500 lb tobo through his
attorney Lt Col An: Elliott. 6 Feb 1653/4. p 138

Puscaticon. See Muster.

Pusie, Eliza. Headright of Jo Paine. 6 Aug 1655. p 209

Raddocke, Richd. Wit Edgecombes public apology to Fantleroy. 15 Sept
1655. p 243

Ratclif, Wm. Headright of Mr Ja Bagnall. 6 Aug 1655. p 208

Raughton see Wraton, Wraughton, etc.

Raven, Peeter. Headright of Capt More Fantleroy. 10 Jan 1652/3. p 27

Rawles, Geo. Wit sale Underwood to Cox. 26 Nov 1653. p 104

Raules, Geo. His a/c incl in settlemt of Lawson est. 20 Jan 1655/6.
p 192

Raules, Geo. Wit Browne to Clapham Sr. 6 June 1655. p 195

Rowles, Geo. Wit assignmt of land Underwood to Moseley. 7th - 1652.
p 214. Also wit assignmt of land Moseley to Fleming. 6 Aug
1655. p 214

Rawlins, Charles. Headright of Capt Wm Brocas. 6 Oct 1652. p 16
Wit: Petterson to Baning. 29 Oct 1652. p 39
Wit: certificate of Will Buttler. No date shown but abt 7 Mar
1652/3. p 46

Rawry. This name not clear. It appears to be "Rauri x Rawry" which
is of course impossible. He appears as a witness in a deed, Geo
Reade to Edmond Kempe. See next entry. 16 May 1654. p 159

Reade, George. Patent. 22 Oct 1651. 600 acres on - side of Peacke-
    tanke river, adj a small creek which divides his land from that
    of Perigrine Bland, etc. George Reade "of the midle plantacon
    in the Countye of Yorke" assigns this land to Edmond Kempe of
    Rappahannock river in Lancaster Co. Wit: Rauri x Rawry (?).
    Roger Ashley. 16 May 1654. p 159. Now follows the most un-
    expected and interesting item in this volume.
    "Cosen Smyth my service presented to you and your wife sir I
    would desire you, on my behalfe to make an acknowledgment in
    your court of a parcell of land sold by me to Mr Kempe as by
    assignmt of my patent will apeare and what you doe hearin shall
    be as Authentick as if I my selfe were present and you shall
    hearin much ingage   Your kinsman and servant
    June the 19th 1653   Geo Reade "   p 159
    (Note: "Cosen Smyth" being Mr. Toby Smyth, Justice of Lancaster
    County. B.F.)

Reding, Rich. Headright of Mr Toby Smith. 6 Aug 1655. p 209
Reddock, Richd. To go peaceably upon the land of Tho Staines and
    fetch away such poultry and hogs as he has there. The poultry
    being 4 hens and a cock. 6 June 1655. p 200
Reddock see Raddocke.
"The Richard and Benjamin of London". Capt Jno Whitty Commander. See
    entry Syth Hayward. 7 March 1653/4. p 142
Richards, Capt Tho. Owes Epa Lawson L 10. Sterling. 13 Apl 1651.p 9
Richards, Wm. Headright of Capt More Fantleroy, 10 Jan 1652/3. p 27
    Richards Creek. On N side Rappa. Adj 681 acres sold by Smyth to
    Webb. 6 Feb 1653/4. p 128
Richardson, Jno. Wit: sale Underwood to Cox. 26 Nov 1653. p 104
Richardson, Rich. Atty of Sym Cuerzee. 8 Dec 1653. p 96
Ridge, Abig: Headright of Mr Toby Smith. 7 Aug 1654. p 151
Ridly, Tho. Wit Hackery to Burroughs. Exact date not shown. It was
    betw 1 Sept 1651 and 16 June 1653. p 148
Rigby, Peeter. (Now here again, this apparently obscure entry has
    to do with the early development of American civilization. Who
    would ever guess that this has to do with the foundations of
    a fortune that developed the greatest financial institution
    that has been in perfect accord with our Government ! Just the
    same, here we are. B.F.)At any event, Peeter Rigby. His land
    on South side of Mulford Haven, adjoins a grant of 500 acres
    to Abraham Moone, See entry his name. 6 June 1650. p 106
Rigby, Peeter. Buys 400 acres on N side Peanoketanck River from
    Rich Lake. See entry his name. 5 Oct 1653. p 107. Also see
    entry Rd Lake, 7 Oct, 1653. p 109.
Rigbey, Mr. (evidently Peter Rigby but still ?) To pay levy on 4
    tytheables to Mr Tho Bourne. 6 Feb 1654/5. p 174
Rigbey, Mr Peeter. Judgt to him agst estate of Rd Lake dec'd for 112
    lb tobo. 6 June 1655. p 198
Rigby, Mr. (Peter) To pay levy on 3 tytheables to Mr Kempe. 7 Dec
    1655. p 239.

Rixham, Xpoffer. And Ann his wife in slander suit. See entry John
  Paine. 6 Aug 1652. p 3
Rixham, Exper. To pay levy on 2 tytheables to Mr Geo Taylor. 6 Feb
  1654/5. p 174
Roberts, Ann. Headright of Edwin Conway. 6 Oct 1652. p 15
Robinson, John and Mary his wife. Complained agst by Capt Thomas
  Hackett for scandal. See entry his name. 8 Dec 1653. p 97
Robinson, Jno. and Wm Sharpe, along with other of his servants com-
  plain of Coll Burbage. 6 Oct 1654. p 163
Robinson, Jno. Judgt to him 400 lb tobo agst est of Tho Steephens.
  6 Feb 1654/5. p 173
  Wit: signature of Mrs Elenor Sharp. 11 Dec 1654. p 187
  To deliver all tobo to Roger Haris for keeping the child of Tho
  Mannah and Eliz Tomlin. 6 June 1655. p 198
  Ordered to pay Jas Gates 600 lb tobo for a cow he bought from
  him. 25 Oct 1655. p 212
  Ordered to pay debt of 550 lb tobo due Capt Hen Fleete. 25th
  Oct 1655. p 212
  To pay Raleigh Travers, atty of Hen Caus-, 681 lb tobo and 1 bu
  corn. 25 Oct 1655. p 212
  He owes Rice Maddocke a cow, challenged by Mr Travers, etc.Is
  ordered to pay Travers 100 lb tobo for the calf, etc. 25 Oct
  1655. p 213
  To pay levy on 1 tytheable to Da: Fox. 7 Dec 1655. p 238
Robinson, Tho. To pay levy on 2 tytheables to Mr Ja Williamson. 6th
  Feb 1654/5. p 174
  To appraise est of Tho Meads dec'd. 6 June 1655. p 197
  To pay levy on 2 tytheables to Mr Wm Underwood. 7 Dec 1655.
  p 234
Rode, David. Headright of Mr Ja Bagnall. 6 Aug 1655. p 208
Roots, Tho. Buys 300 acres on E side Farnham Creek from More Fantle-
  roy. 8 July 1652. p 7
  Ordered to refund Joane the relict of Hen: Lee 100 lb tobo
  overpd. 10 Jan 1652/3. p 26
  Wit Rice Jones to Petterson. 22 Oct 1652. p 39
  Wit: Coleman to Mascall. No date shown. Prior to 1653. pp 54-5
  Wit: deed Brice to Paine. 25 July 1653. p 67
  Owes Wm Clapham Sr 660 lb tobo. 6 Oct 1653. p 79
  Certificate for land for his own transportation into this
  colony. 8 Dec 1653. p 97
  Is assigned debt 100 lb tobo due from Jas Yates to Mr Edwwin
  Conaway. 9 Dec 1653. p 99
  Pre-nuptial agreement. 14 Oct 1653. Tho Roots of Lancaster Co.,
  Chirurgeon, and Fra Attawell, daughter of Mar: Grimes widow. To
  be married. Regards cattle "given to her by her father Attawell"
  (Tho Adawell). Wit: Edwin Conaway. Wm White. p 121
  He assigns 300 acres to Marg Grimes widow of Edw Grimes for
  life. Wit: James Williamson. Peet'r Knight. 8 Dec 1653. p 122
  Judgt agst him for 750 lb tobo to Major J Carter assignee of
  Exper Asshley and Jno Best. 6 Feb 1653/4. p 139

Roots, Tho. Attachmt to him agst est of Danl Jones for debt 300 lb
    tobo. 6 Feb 1654/5. p 173
    To pay levy on 1 tytheable to Mr Tho Brice. 6 Feb 1654/5. p 174
    Wit assignmt of land Roughton to Brathat. 25 Oct 1655. p 215
    Entry shows him as 'Chyrurgeon'. P of A to him from his brother
    Wm Roughton. 24 Oct 1655. p 215
Rosier, Rev. John. (He was of Westmoreland Co at this period) In this
    entry as 'Mr Jno Rosier cler''. The dif betw him and Thos Wills
    mate of Capt Throwgoods ship "is rest to the 6th day of 10'ber
    next beinge the Court daye for this County". 6 June 1655. p 196
Roughton, William. Assigns Jno Brathat all int in a grant. Does not
    state what grant. Wit Tho Roots. 25 Oct 1655. Recorded 10 Nov
    1655. p 215
    Entry shows him of Lancaster Co., planter. P of A to his well
    beloved brother Tho Roots of Va., Chyrurgeon, to transact
    business in his name. Wit Vin Stanford. 24 Oct 1655. p 215
    He assigns Jno Brathett all interest in 300 acres, part of a
    dividend of 400 acres formerly surveyed for Richd Flint and
    himself. Wit: Abra Moune. Jno Edwards. 27 Sept 1655. p 216
Roughton see Wraughton.
Rowsey, Mr. To pay levy on 6 tytheables to Mr Lucas. 7 Dec 1655.
    p 238
Rowsee, Ralfe. His land on S side Rappa adj a patent of Tho Lucas.
    7 Aug 165- (blotted, prior to 1654). p 220
Rowze, Mr. To pay levy on 8 tytheables to Mr Andrew Gilson. 24 Oct
    1653. p 94
Rowles, Mary. Headright of Wm Tigner. 6 Apl 1653. p 43
Rowsey, Tho. To pay levy on 1 tytheable to Mr Felson. 7 Dec 1655.
    p 238
Royes Nest. Was Fauntleroy home in Nansemum Co. See entry Toby
    Smith. 29 Sept 1647. pp 81-2
Rye, Hen. To give evidence re Toby Horton's lending guns to Indians.
    6 June 1654. p 146
    To pay levy on 2 tytheables to Maj Jno Carter. 6 Feb 1654/5.
    p 174
    To pay levy on 1 tytheable to Maj Jo Carter. In this entry as
    Rie. 7 Dec 1655. p 234

St Johns Creek. Grant of 560 acres to John Meredith, shipwright, on
    West side of this creek. 10 Oct 1652. p 134
St Mary's White Chapel. See Fox family memo.
Sachell, Eliz: Headright of Mr Row Lawson. 6 Feb 1654/5. p 172
Sacks, Thos. Elected Constable from lower side of Corotowomen River
    downwards on the North. 6 Aug 1653. p 62
    See entry Wm Newsam et als. 29 Jan 1649/50. p 69
Sargan, Fra: Headright of Jno Gillet. 6 Oct 1654. p 162
Saxton, Nich. Headright of Sir H Chisley. 10 Jan 1652/3. p 27
Scapes, Jno. Wit Bennett-Clapham-Lawson transaction. 12 Sept 1652.
    p 31

Seamor, Thomas. Binds himself to pay Tho Carter 1095 lb tobo at the
    house of Tobyas Horton next October, or all the tobo he shall
    make in the year 1653. Wit Tho Madestard. Eby Bonison. 16 Mar
    1652/3. p 47

Seapes, Jno. Wit bond Epa Lawson to Rd Bennett. 13 Apl 1651. p 9

Seden, Jno. Headright of Wm Brocas. 6 Oct 1652. p 16

Segar, Oliver. Certificate for land for his own transportation into
    the Colony. 6 Aug 1653. p 62
    To be pd from levy for 2 wolves' heads. 6 Oct 1653. p 78
    To pay levy on 2 tytheables to Mr Rd Perrot. To be pd 300 lb
    tobo from levy by Mr Perrot for 2 wolves heads. 24 Oct 1653.
    p 93
    His estate attached at suit of Wm Lynell and Hen Dedman. 6 Apl
    1654. p 140
    To pay levy on 2 tytheables to Mr Rd Perrott. 6 Feb 1654/5.
    p 174
    To be pd 750 lb tobo from est of Paule Brewer dec'd for funeral
    charges and to be pd before any other debt. 6 June 1655. p 197

Seniour, Mr Jno. His land on upper N.W. side of Corotomen River adj
    Thos Hackett. 25 Oct 1655. p 226

Sewell, Fran. Headright of Wm Clapham Jr. 6 June 1654. p 145

Sharpe, Mr. To pay levy on 14 tytheables to Mr Da Fox. 6th Febry
    1654/5. p 174
    To pay levy on 13 tytheables to Da: Fox. 7 Dec 1655. p 238

Sharpe, Hen. Headright of Mr Rd Perrott. 6 Oct 1653. p 77

Sharpe, Jno. Judgt confessed to him by Wm Downman for 2000 lb tobo.
    10 Jan 1652/3. p 26
    Judgt confessed by him as atty of John Hunt, admr of Geo Eaton,
    for a month's work of an able hand to John Meriman. 6 Apl 1653.
    p 44
    To pay levy on 6 tytheables to Mr Da Fox. 24 Oct 1653. p 91
    Attorney of Jno Hunt. See entry Jno Eaton. 8 Dec 1653. p 97
    Buys 300 acres on Grymes Creek from Tho Harwood. 26 June 1651.
    p 119
    Is assigned 200 acres at Fleets Bay by Capt Hen Fleet. No date
    but recorded 10 Dec 1653. p 132
    Security for Jno Meredith and Walter Herd admrs of Mrs Frances
    Edmonds decd. 7 Mar 1653/4. p 142
    Elected Constable. 6 June 1654. p 146
    Buys 200 acres in Fleets Bay from Capt Hen Fleet after 1 Aug
    1652. He sold it to Hugh Brent. Dower rights relinq by Elenor
    Sharp wife of Jno. 11 Dec 1654. p 186
    Wit Lawson to Lawson. 6 June 1655. p 205
    Wit deed Powell to Downman. 19 Nov 1652. p 216
    Entry states he is husband of Elinor Denhawes (also as Denham).
    See entry Tho Hackett. 25 Oct 1655. p 226

Sharpe, Wm. He with Jno Robinson and other of his servants complain
    of Coll Burbage. 6 Oct 1654. p 163

Shaw, Eliza: Headright of Geo Taylor. 6 Oct 1654. p 162

Sheare, Geo. Headright of Capt More Fantleroy. 10 Jan 1652/3. p 27

Sheares, Wm. See entry Wm Lea. 20 Sept 1649. p 5

    See entry Tho Whettell. 11 May 1651. p 6

Shepheard, Abraham. Wit P of A Jno Shepheard of Rotterdam to his brother Wm Harris. See entry Hen Montford. 12 Aug 1650. p 83

Shepheard, John of Roterdam, merchant. P of A to "his welbeloved brother Wm Harris" to rec a/cs from Wm Underwood and James Williamson, merchants. 12 Aug 1650. p 84

Sherlock, Jno. Certificate for land for transportation of 3 persons into the Colony. 24 Oct 1653. p 89

    To pay levy on 2 tytheables to Mr Toby Smith. 24 Oct 1653.p 92

    Dif betw him and Wm Price to next Court. 6 Feb 1654/5. p 173

    His a/c incl in settlemt of Lawson estate. 20 Jan 1655/6.p 192

    To view house built by Jno Edgecomb for Capt Fantleroy and report. 6 June 1655. p 199

    Security for Tho Walker. 6 June 1655. p 200

    To pay levy on 2 tytheables to Mr Wm Underwood. 7 Dec 1655. p 234

Shirt, Wm. Headright of Mr Tho Carter. 6 Feb 1654/5. p 172

Shuldrun, Hen. Headright of Capt Hen Fleet. 6 June 1655. p 198

Simpson, Da: Headright of Mr Richd Perrott. 6 Oct 1653. p 77

Ssisson, Robt. (sic) Headright of Jno Sherlock. 24 Oct 1653. p 89

Skipwith, Diana. Wit mortgage Tho Carter to Jno Carter. 18 Sep 1655. p 228

Sladen, Marie. Headright of Mr Ja Bagnell. 6 Aug 1655. p 208

Slaughter, Jno. His land on N side Rappa abt 10 miles up. Adjs a patent of 1000 acres of Epa Lawson. 22 Feb 1650/1. p 34

Slaughter's Creek. See entry Epa Lawson. 3 Sept 1649. p 33. Also referred to as abt 8 miles up the Rappa. 12 July 1654. p 188

Slight, Geo. Headright of Rice Jones. 6 Aug 1652. p 2

Sleight, Geo. Wit Jones to Powell. 8 Jan 1652/3. p 51

    Wit Powell to Haris. 12 Jan 1652/3. p 52

Sloper, Saml. Formerly leased land from Wm Clapham on a neck adj 700 acres sold by Clapham to Capt Hen Fleet. 30 June 1655. p 229

Smart, Mr. To pay levy to Mr Geo Taylor thus "Mr Smart himselfe 2 seamen servants his overseer Carpenter Lattr Capt other servt and 2 that he hired of Wm Yarrett". 10 tytheables. 24 Oct 1653. p 92

Smart, Wm. See entry Mr Tho Hawkins. 6 Aug 1655. p 209

Smith, John. Headright of Sir H Chisley. 10 Jan 1652/3. p 27

Smyth, Jno. His land on S side Mulford Haven. Adjs grant 500 acres to Abra Moone. 6 June 1650. p 106

Smyth, Jno. Headright of Mr And Gilson. 6 Oct 1654. p 162

Smyth, Mark. Headright of Mr Tho Carter. 6 Feb 1654/5. p 172

Smyth, Mary. Headright of Mr Tho Carter. 6 Feb 1654/5. p 172

Smith, Richd. Headright of David Fox. 6 Oct 1652. p 15

Smith, Tho. Headright of Wm Tigner. 6 Apl 1653. p 43

Smith, Mr Toby. Justice. 1 July 1652. p 1

    Justice. 6 Aug 1652. p 2

    Wit deed Fantleroy to Roots. 8 July 1652. p 7

Smith, Mr Toby. Land assigned to him by More Fantleroy. 200 acres
in Rappa abt 44 miles up on S side. To "my brother in law Toby
Smith gent" and heirs begotten of Phebe his wife. (Mrs Smith
was Phebe Fantleroy and sister of Capt More Fantleroy). 24 Oct
1651. p 12
See 2 entries in More Fantleroy's name this date. 24 Oct 1651.
p 13
Justice. 6 Oct 1652. p 15
Certificate for land for importing 7 persons into the Colony.
6 Oct 1652. p 16
Justice. 10 Jan 1652/3. p 23
Letter from Ri Bennett regarding Wm Clapham and the Lawson
estate. Dated Rappa River 12 Sept 1652. p 32
A Court held at his house. 6 Apl 1653. p 43
Statemt sworn before him as Justice. 24 Feb 1652/3. p 45
P of A from Denis Coniers. See entry his name. 26 Mar 1653.
p 50
He and Mr Rich Loes give a heifer to "Henry Wm'son sun in Law
to the said Mr Loes". Recorded 6 Aug 1653. p 58
Justice. 6 Aug 1653. p 61
Justice. 6 Oct 1653. p 77
To report on boundries betw Tho Paine and Hen Dedman. 6th Oct
1653. p 78
Entry refers to him as Toby Smyth of Nansemum in the Collony
of Virginia Gent. For certain considerations received "of my
brother in law More Fantleroy" of Royes rest in the County of
Nansemum, Gent., and for natural love and affection for "my
sonne Toby and Daughter Phoebe" about last April gave the
children 3 cattle, etc. The boy under 21 and the girl under 18,
only children and their mother living. 29 Sept 1647. Witnesses
Anthony Buck, George Gwilliam, Sarah Parsons. Recorded in Lanc
Co. 10 Oct 1653. Phebe Smyth states the 3 cattle were in ex-
change for a parcel of land situated at Nutmegquarter made over
for her and her children and is with consent of her brother
More Fantleroy. 10 Sept 1653. Wit: John Carter, David Fox and
Rowland Lawson. pp 81-2
Justice. 24 Oct 1653. p 89
To collect levy on 35 tytheables incl 3 tytheables of his own.
24 Oct 1653. p 91
Justice. 8 Dec 1653. p 96
His servant, Mary Smyth, punished for having a bastard child,
absenting herself from service contrary to orders from Mr Jas
Wm'son and "for sundry slighting languages". 9 Dec 1653. p 98
Deed. 6 Feb 1653/4. Major John Carter on behalf of Toby Smith
sells Gyles Webb 681 acres on N side Rappa river on Richards
Creek and 400 acres on S side Rappa river, etc. Wit: John
Phillips. Rich Loes. p 128
Justice. 16 May 1654. p 131
Wit: Fleet to Sharpe. 10 Dec 1653. p 132
P of A from Lambert Lambertson. 31 Jan 1653/4. p 135

Smith, Mr Toby. Justice. 6 Feb 1653/4. p 137
    To survey land of Abra Weekes on petition of Da: Wealch. 6 Feb
    1653/4. p 138
    Justice. 6 Apl 1654. p 140
    Certificate for land for importing 9 persons into the Colony.
    7 Aug 1654, p 151
    Justice. 7 Aug 1654. p 151
    See entry Geo Reade who writes to him as "Cosen Smyth". 19 June
    1653. p 157
    Justice. 6 Oct 1654. p 162
    Arrests Sebastian Powlinge in debt of 593 1b tobo. 6 Oct 1654.
    p 163
    Judgt to him as attorney for Capt Jno Whitty for 465 1b tobo
    agst the estate of Rd Lake dec'd. 6 Oct 1654. p 163
    Justice. 6 Feb 1654/5. p 171
    His name with that of Mr Ja: Bagnall and Mr David Fox presented
    to the Governor and Council for election of Sheriff. 6th Feb
    1654/5. p 172
    To collect levy on 26 tytheables incl 6 tytheables of his own
    family. 6 Feb 1654/5. p 174
    Wit deed Fleet to Sharp. No date but betw 1 Aug 1652 and 11 Dec
    1654. p 186
    Justice. 7 May 1655. p 189
    Certifies schedule of Capt Wm Brocas' estate. Recorded 7 May
    1655. p 191
    His a/c incl in settlemt of Lawson estate. 20 Jan 1655/6.p 192
    Judgmt to him, as atty of Capt Jno Whitty, for 1016 1b of
    "bisquite" to be pd by Geo Kibble admr of est of Rd Lake dec'd.
    6 June 1655. p 198
    Certificate for land for importing 3 persons into this Colony.
    6 Aug 1655. p 209
    P of A from Capt John Whitty. 19 May 1654. p 222
    To receive levy on 23 tytheables from 7 persons incl 7 tythea-
    bles for himself. 7 Dec 1655. p 239
Smither, Jno. Wit deed Lake to Kibble. 7 Oct 1653. p 109
Smythson, Tho. Headright of Da: Felps. 6 Feb 1653/4. p 139
Snead, Charles. He and Eliz Wig confess "of the odious sin of
    fornicacon". 6 Aug 1652. p 3
    Half of 300 acres bought by Tho Powell and Jno Paine from Wm
    Clapham belongs to him, he having bought Paine's half. 5 Dec
    1652. p 48
    Is assigned 1/2 interest in 408 acres by Howell Powell. See
    entry Geo Haris. 14 Mar 1652/3. p 52
    Is assigned by Howell Powell his interest in 320 acres on N
    side of Rappa. 5 Mar 1652/3. pp 54-5
    Is assigned interest in a patent by John Paine. 21 Oct 1654.
    p 183
Snooke, Jno. Came to this country with indentures for 10 yrs. See
    entry Will Buttler. 28 Sept 1652. p 46
Sparon, Wm. Headright of Dominick Theriott. 6 Oct 1652. p 16

Spencer, Alice. Headright of Clemt Thrush. 6 Oct 1652. p 15
Springe, Robt. Headright of Toby Smith. 6 Oct 1652. p 16
Squib, Jno. Ordered to pay Wm Thomas 30 lb tobo for loss of 2 days
   time as a witness. 7 Aug 1654. p 152
Staines, Tho. To deliver poultry and hogs belonging to Rd Reddock.
   6 June 1655. p 200
Staines, Mr. To pay levy on 5 tytheables to Mr Griffin. 7 Dec 1655.
   p 236
Staines, Tho. To pay levy on 6 tytheables to Mr Toby Smith. 6 Feby
   1654/5. p 174
Stainingbrcw, Jno. Headright of Mr Andı Gilson. 6 Oct 1654. p 162
Stanford, Vinc. Wit Herd to Carter. 1 Apl 1657. This date is correct.
   The item is out of order in records. 1 Apl 1657. p 130
   Wit deed Paine to Snead. 21 Oct 1654. p 183
   Wit deed Best to Williams and Porteus. 5 Feb 1654/5. p 184
   Buys 300 acres on N side Peacketanke River from Jno Ashley and
   Tho Hamper, 10 Sept 1654. p 188
   Certificate for land for transportation of 5 persons. 6 June
   1655. p 198
   Attachmt to him agst est of Humphrie Haggett for fees, etc. 25
   Oct 1655. p 211
   Wit P of A Roughton to Roots. 24 Oct 1655. p 215
   Appears in records as Clerk. 1 Dec 1655. p 217
   As Clerk 1 Nov 1655. p 221
   Wit Herd to Meredith. 16 May 1655. p 227
   Deed recorded by him 25 Oct 1655. p 229
   Ordered to deliver Jo Meredith's bill 450 lb tobo to Tho Bush-
   rode. 7 Dec 1655. p 231
   The County to pay him 1500 lb tobo "for his paine in severall
   imploymts". 7 Dec 1655. p 234
   To receive levy on 26 tytheables from 9 persons. 7 Dec 1655.
   p 235
Staples, Joane. Headright of Tho Paine. 6 Oct 1652. p 15
Stevens, Mr. To pay levy on 4 tytheables to Da: Fox. 7 Dec 1655.
   p 238
Stevens, Mr. Formerly bought land from Wm Clapham on a neck adj 700
   acres sold by Clapham to Capt Hen Fleet. 30 June 1655. p 229
Steephens, Anth: Wit Welch to Coopland. 6 June 1655. p 194
Steephens, Magda and Mary, Headrights of Jno Weir. 6 Oct 1654.p 162
Steephens, Rich. To pay levy on 1 tytheable to Mr Geo Taylor. 24th
   Oct 1653. p 92
Steephens, Tho. Deceased. Admr of his est to Elizabeth his relict.
   7 Aug 1654. p 153
   His estate to be appraised by Mr Ja: Bagnall, Mr Rice Jones,
   Mr Tho Griffin and Mr Tho Paine. 7 Aug 1654. p 153
   Judgt agst his est to Jno Robinson for 400 lb tobo. 6th Feby
   1654/5. p 173
Stevenson, Tho. Headright of Tobie Horton. 6 Aug 1655. p 208
Steephenson, Jno. Buys 700 acres from Wm Clapham Jr. 12 July 1654.
   p 188

Steephenson, Edw. Headright twice of Mr Rich Leake. 6 Feb 1653/4.
p 139

Steale, Ellen. Headright of Clemt: Thrush. 6 Oct 1652. p 15

Streator, Capt Tho., who married the widow of Col Burbage, is sued
by Rev. Phillip Mallory guardian of Tho Oldis. 17 March 1657/8.
Northumberland Co records. No.15, p 4.

Sullivan, Marie. Shown in entry as 'Marie Sallivon'. Headright of
Mr Edmond Kemp. 25 Oct 1655. p 213

Sunderland Creek. Referred to 5 Mar 1651/2. p 118
It adjs land of Hen Nicholls, Denis Coniers and Evan Davies.
29 July 1652, p 157
Is on S side Rappa: see Welch to Coopland. 6 June 1655. p 194

Swan, Wm. Headright of Mr Toby Smith. 7 Aug 1654, p 151

Symon, Eliz. Headright of Capt Hen Fleet. 6 June 1655. p 198

Taberery, Tho. (This name is not Tho Zakerery). Wit agreemt Nicholas
and Nicholls. 13 June 1653. p 115

Talbot, Wm. Headright of Mr Toby Smith. 7 Aug 1654. p 151

Tapley, Geo. Wit Sharpe to Dudley et als. 6 Feb 1651/2. p 119

Taverner, - and his wife. Ref to in letter of Nickloas George. See
that entry. 30 Oct 1652. p 36

Taylor, Mr. Ordered to pay 300 lb tobo to Jno Weir exor of Robert
Chambers, for use of sloop from James River. Sil Thatcher to
pay 600 lb tobo for same. 6 Aug 1655. p 209

Taylor, Mr. To pay levy on 6 tytheables to Jno Paine. 7 Dec 1655.
p 239

Taylor also appears as Taler.

Taylor, An. Headright of Fra Gower. 24 Oct 1653. p 89

Taylor, Mr George. Justice. 1 July 1652. p 1
Justice. 6 Aug 1652. p 2
Justice. 6 Oct 1652. p 15
To appraise est of Robt Viman dec'd. 6 Oct 1652. p 16 (Vivian)
Justice. 10 Jan 1652/3, p 23
Appraises the good of Mr Robt Vivran dec'd. 12 Jan 1652/3. p 38
See entry 'Muster'. 8 Aug 1653. p 65
Justice. 6 Aug 1653. p 61
Justice. 6 Oct 1653. p 77
To collect levy on 24 tytheables from 5 persons incl 6 for
himself. 24 Oct 1653. p 92
He owes 180 lb tobo on a/c to the estate of Robt Vivian dec'd.
10 Feb 1653/4. p 117
Justice. 6 Apl 1654. p 140
Certificate for land for importing 4 persons into this Colony.
6 Oct 1654. p 162
Justice, 6 Oct 1654. p 162
To be pd 300 lb tobo by Jno Weir exor of Robt Chambers. 6 Oct
1654. p 162
Patent. Dated last of Jan 1653/4. 300 acres on N side Rappa
adj his own land by a former grant. He assigns this 300 acres
to Mathyas Tomlin. Wit Jno Phillips, Andrew Gilson. 6th Oct
1654. p 166

Taylor, Mr George. To collect levy on 24 tytheables incl 3 of his
own family. 6 Feb 1654/5. p 174
   Justice. A Court held at his house. His name is entered here
   as 'Mr Georg Taler'. 6 Aug 1655. p 207
   Justice. A Court at his house. 7 Dec 1655. p 233
   His land adjs 760 acres patented by Jno Bond. See entry his
   name. 29 Feb 1650/1. p 240
Taylor, Jno. Deceased. Admr to Elizabeth his relict. 10 Jan 1652/3.
   p 24
   His widow Elizabeth sued by Col Wm Clayborne Esqr. Dismissed.
   Nonsuit to her. 6 Apl 1653. p 43
Taylor, Jno. To pay levy on 3 tytheables to Maj Jno Carter. 6th Feb
   1654/5. p 174
Taylor, John. Headright of Jo: Eyers. 6 Aug 1655. p 208
Taylor, Jo: To pay levy to V Stanford. 7 Dec 1655. p 235
Taylor, Peeter. Dif betw him and Wm Jonson to next Court. 6th Oct
   1653. p 78
   His a/c incl in settlemt of Lawson estate. 20 Jan 1655/6. p 192
Tennies, Edw. Appraises est of Wm Foote dec'd. 10 Jan 1652/3. p 23
Thacker. A cow named this at this date. 7 May 1653. p 68
Thatcher, Wm. Was arrested at suit of Elias Edmonds and did not
   appear. Judgt agst Wm Clapham Sr his security. 6 Apl 1653. p 43
   Is ordered to pay Elias Edmonds 1000 lb tobo for killing his
   hogs contrary to law. 8 Aug 1653. p 63
   To pay levy on 2 tytheables to Mr Row Lawson. 24 Oct 1653. p 90
Thatcher, Sil: (Silvester). To pay levy on 3 tytheables to Mr Geo
   Taylor. 6 Feb 1654/5. p 174
   Fails to prosecute Jno Weir in suit. 6 June 1655. p 199
   Nonsuited in action agst Jno Weir. 6 Aug 1655. p 208
   Certificate for land for importing 4 persons into this Colony.
   6 Aug 1655. p 208
   Mrs Thatcher complains that in her husband's absence 2 servants
   were away 2 months. The servants ordered to serve 3 mos beyond
   their time. 7 March 1664/5. p 209
   Sued by Jno Weir, exor of Robt Chambers, for use of sloop from
   James River. Ordered to pay 600 lb tobo. Mr Taylor ordered to
   pay 300 lb tobo. 6 Aug 1655. p 209
   To pay levy on 3 tytheables to Jno Paine. 7 Dec 1655. p 239
Thatchwell, Willm. To pay levy on 2 tytheables to Abra Weekes. 7th
   Dec 1655. p 237
Theriott, Dominick. This person was a French gentleman. Monsieur
   however you care to spell it. Dominick, Domino, Domine not to
   mention Cheriott, Theriott, Theriot, Therriot, Therriott, etc.
   At any event here we are:
   Certificate for land for importing 3 persons into this Colony.
   6 Oct 1652. p 16
   Admr of estate of Epa Lawson to him to pay debt of 3400 lb tobo.
   6 Oct 1652. p 16
   He married the relict of Hen Lee. Com of admr of Lee's estate
   to him. 10 Jan 1652/3. p 23

Therriott, Dominick. The balance of Epa Lawson's estate to be deliv-
ered to him after Mr Jno Carter has been pd 7067 lb tobo. 10th
Jan 1652/3. p 23
  Dif betw him and Abra Moone to next Court. 10 Jan 1652/3. p 26
  Admr of Hen Lee dec'd. See entry Abra Moone. 6 Aug 1653. p 61
  Assigns a debt of 3400 lb tobo to Robt Mascall. See entry his
  name. 6 Aug 1653. p 62
  Will give evidence in case of debt Howes vs White. 26 May 1653.
  p 87
  Entered simply as 'Dominick'. To pay levy on 4 tytheables to
  Mr Tho Brice. 24 Oct 1653. p 91
  His business to next Court. Da: Jones to put in security to
  appear. 7 Aug 1654. p 152
  Fined 2000 lb tobo for lending a gun to an Indian. Wm Denby who
  delivered the gun to pay 700 lb of the fine. Half to be paid to
  Daniel Jones who informed. Major John Carter and Wm Clapham Jr
  to have 30 lb tobo each for hire of 2 men to guard the house
  of Marga: Grimes "on the Death of the Indyan" from whom the gun
  was taken. 6 Oct 1654. p 163
  Entered merely as 'Domine'. To pay levy on 4 tytheables to Mr
  Tho Brice. 6 Feb 1654/5. p 174
  In this entry as 'Mons'r Therryott'. To pay levy on 3 tytheables to Wm Neesham. 7 Dec 1655. p 237
Thomas, Joane. Wife of Wm Thomas. Arrested at suit of Mr Tho Griffin
  for slander on him and Sarah the wife of John Phillips. She is
  ordered to publicly acknowledge her offence agst Mr Griffin
  "the next time that the minister officiates in the upper parts
  of the river" and to acknowledge her offence agst Mrs Sarah
  Phillips "the next Lords day when the minister shall officiate
  in the lower parts of the river". 9 Dec 1653. p 99. (Note: We
  do not know who Mr Thos Griffin's wife was other than her name
  was Sarah. John Phillips was dead 1655. What of that ? BF)
Thomas, Miles and Roy. Headrights of Sill Thatcher. 6 Aug 1655.p 208
Thomas, Rob. Headright of Capt Hen Fleet. 24 Oct 1653. p 89
Thomas, Wm. Suit agst him by Mr Tho Brice dismissed. 6 Oct 1652.p 15
  He and Jone his wife. All suits agst est of Mr Tho Brice decd
  to next Court. 6 Oct 1652. p 15
  Certificate for land for importing Joan Bayley into this Colony.
  10 Jan 1652/3. p 24
  Ordered to pay debt of 711 lb tobo due Mr Tho Brice. 10th Jan
  1652/3. p 27
  Wit: P of A dated 14 Jan 1650/1 Harris to Astell. See entry Hen
  Monford. p 83
  To be pd 30 lb tobo as witness for Jno Squibb. 7 Aug 1654.p 152
  Dif betw him and Jno Phillips to next Court. 6 Oct 1654. p 164
  Attachmt agst his estate to Wm Wraughton for 200 lb tobo and
  4 shillings Sterling. 6 Oct 1654. p 164
Thompson also appears as Tompson.
Thompson, Richd (signed with mark). Wit deed Haggett to Hill. 12th
  Apl 1655. p 207

Thompson, Robt. To pay levy on 2 tytheables to Wm Neesham. 7th Dec.
　　1655. p 237
Thompson, Wm. To pay levy on 3 tytheables to Mr Rd Perrott. 6 Feby
　　1654/5. p 174
　　To pay levy on 2 tytheables to Abrs Weekes. 7 Dec 1655. p 237
Thorpe, John. Headright of Capt Wm Brocas. 6 Oct 1652. p 16
Thorpe, Tho. Headright of Da Felps. 6 Feb 1653/4. p 139
Thouninge, Robt. Headright of Sir H Chisley. 10 Jan 1652/3. p 27
Throwgood, Capt. The mate of his ship, Tho Wills, in dif with Rev.
　　Jno Rosier. 6 June 1655. p 196
Thrush, Clemt. Certificate for 300 acres for importing 6 persons. 6
　　Oct 1652. p 15
　　Petitions for admr of est of Robt Viman decd as by his will.Jno
　　Gillett ordered to deliver what he has of the est to Mr George
　　Taylor and Mr An Gilson for appraisal. (This name is actually
　　Robt Vivian). 6 Oct 1652. p 16
　　To have admr of est of Robert Vivian late of Lancaster Co by
　　order from Ri Bennett, Governor, etc. 10 Dec 1652. p 35
　　As admr of Robt Vivian dec'd ordered to file inventory. 6 Oct
　　1653. p 80
　　To pay levy on 3 tytheables to Mr And Gilson. 24 Oct 1653.p 94
　　Wit P of A Paine to Travers. 6 Dec 1653. p 103
　　Owes est of Robt Vivian decd 541 lb tobo, also by a/c 300 lb
　　tobo. 10 Feb 1653/4. p 117
　　To pay levy on 6 tytheables to Mr And Gilson. 6 Feb 1654/5.
　　p 174
　　To appraise est of Paul Brewer. 6 June 1655. p 201
　　To pay levy on 4 tytheables to Mr Felson. 7 Dec 1655. p 238
Trush, Fras Headright of Jno Gillet. 6 Oct 1654. p 162
Tignall, Mr. To pay levy on 7 tytheables to Mr Jno Cox. 6 Feb 1654/5
　　p 174
Tigner, Mr. To pay levy on 5 tytheables to Mr Jno Cox. 24 Oct 1653.
　　p 93
Tigner, Wm. Certificate for land for transportation of 6 persons
　　into this colony. 6 Apl 1653. p 43
　　Buys 300 acres on S side Rappa from Jas Bonner. 6 June 1654.
　　p 147
Tignoll, Mr. To pay levy on 8 tytheables to Wm Leech. 7 Dec 1655.
　　p 236
Tilsley, Tho. Headright of V Stanford. 6 June 1655. p 198
Tomlin, Mr. To pay levy on 6 tytheables to Mr And Gilson. 24th Oct
　　1653. p 94
Tomlyn, Mr. To pay levy on 4 tytheables to Mr Felson. 7 Dec 1655.
　　p 238
Tomlyn, Eliza. On her petition Mr Tho Griffin is ordered to pay her
　　"29 lb cotton a smock a pair of shoes and stokins and 3 bar'lls
　　of corne and her bed and Chest given her in the time of her
　　service". Also an order regarding a hhd of tobo left by Tho
　　Mannaugh with Mr Griffin toward keeping the child "by him be-
　　gotten on the said Eliza Tomlin". Also that she be punished.
　　6 Feb 1653/4. p 138

...iza: Her child by Tho Mannah to be kept by Roger Haris and
...ife till 18. Haris to have all the tobo from Jno Robinson,
6 June 1655. p 198

Tomlyn, Mathyas. Buys 300 acres on N side Rappa from Geo Taylor. 6th
Oct 1654. p 166

Tomlyn, Robt. Dif betw him and Jno Gillet to next Court. 6 Oct 1653.
p 77

Certificate for land to him for importing 3 persons into this
Colony. 6 Oct 1653. p 78

Dif betw him and Jno Gellet to next Court. 9 Dec 1653. p 101

Suit agst him by Robt Moss to next Court. 6 Apl 1654. p 140

Tomblin, Rob: Suit agst him by Jno Gillett dismissed for non-appear-
ance. 6 Apl 1654. p 141

Tomlines, Robt. Wit deed Gillet to Greene. 6 Oct 1654. p 167

Tomlin, Mr Robt. Appeals to General Court regarding land dif with
Mr An: Gilson. 6 Feb 1654/5. p 171

To pay levy on 4 tytheables to Mr And: Gilson. 6 Feb 1654/5.
p 174

Tomlinson, Rich. To pay levy on 1 tytheable to Mr Wm Underwood. 7th
Dec 1655. p 234

Top, Michael. Wit P of A Harris to Astell. See entry Hen Monford. 12
Aug 1650. and 14 Jan 1650/1. p 83

Tope, Jere. Headright of Capt Hen Fleet. 24 Oct 1653. p 89

Totoskey Creek. See Muster. 8 Aug 1653. 65

Towers, Jno. Pd 210 lb tobo from Co levy. Does not show what for.
10 Jan 1652/3. p 29

Townsend, Capt. He and Mr Row Burnham sold 6 negroes to Sir Henry
Chicheley. 10 Jan 1652/3. p 27

Travers, Raleigh. Headright of Jno Cable. 6 Oct 1653. p 79

Travers, Mr Raleigh. Has P of A from Tho Paine to implead Captain
Fantleroy. 6 Dec 1653. p 103

Mr Jno Paine and Nich: Forman to 'vew' (view) his tobo house
and report to this Court. 6 Feb 1654/5. p 172

Ordered to pay James Nicolls 3 hhd tobo for wages. 6 Feb 1654/5.
p 172

To be pd 115 lb tobo by Tho Williams. 6 Feb 1654/5. p 172

To pay levy on 7 tytheables to Mr Da: Fox. 6 Feb 1654/5. p 174

In this entry as 'Ralelf Travers'. As atty of Hen: Caus- to be
pd debt of 681 lb tobo and 1 bu Indian corn by Jno Robinson. 25
Oct 1655. p 212

In dif with Jno Robinson regarding a cow and debt of 681 lb tobo
and 1 bu corn. 25 Oct 1655. pp 212-13

To pay levy on 6 tytheables to Da Fox. 7 Dec 1655. p 238

Turnor, Sara. Headright of Mr Row Lawson. 6 Feb 1654/5. p 172

Underwood, Mr Wm. Justice. 1 July 1652. p 1

Justice, 10 Jan 1652/3. p 23

He and Capt Hen Fleet pd 3305 lb tobo from County levy. Does
not state what for. 10 Jan 1652/3. p 29

See entry 'Muster'. 8 Aug 1653. p 65

Underwood, Mr Wm. Justice. 6 Oct 1653. p 77
    Now dwelling in Virginia. See entry Hen Montford. 12 Aug 1650.
    p 83. Also on p 84 where he is ref to as Wm Underwood, merchant.
    To pay levy on 5 tytheables to Mr Toby Smyth. 24 Oct 1653.p 92
    He sells Jno Cox 2 cows. Wit: Jno Richardson. Geo: Rawles. 26th
    Nov 1653. p 104
    Ref to as of Lancaster Co. Sells Tho Meads 700 acres, half of a
    patent of 1400 acres, above the land of Mr Jas Williamson, etc.
    Wit: Ric Loes. Jno Phillips. 12 Sept 1653. p 111
    Justice. 6 Feb 1654/5. p 171
    Justice. 6 June. 1655. p 196
    Administers oath to appraisore of Tho Mead's est. 6 June 1655.
    p 197
    Order that he build Court House on land adj his house. 6 June
    1655. p 201
    Justice. 6 Aug 1655. p 207
    Guardian of Tho Mead orphan of Tho Meads decd. 6 Aug 1655.p 209
    He assigns interest in a patent to Wm Moosley. Teste George
    Rowles. 7th - 1652. Wm Moesley of Lancaster Co assigns this
    land to Elex Fleming. Test Geo Rowles. Recorded IV day of 9ber
    1655 per me Vin: Stanford. The assignmt Loesley to Fleming 6th
    Aug 1655. p 214
    Wit deed Meade to Doerders (ancestor of Minor family). 17th
    Nov 1653. p 221. (He signs as 'Willi Underwood')
    Justice. 7 Dec 1655. p 231
    To be guardian of Thos Meades son of Thos Meads decd. The whole
    estate of Meads, now in the hands of Geo Bries, to be delivered
    to Mr Underwood. 7 Dec 1655. p 233
    The County is indebted to "Mr Underwood for provisions in the
    March 0150" lb tobo. 7 Dec 1655. p 233
    To receive levy from 10 persons on 28 tytheables incl 6 for
    himself. 7 Dec 1655. p 234
    The next Court for the upper part of the County to be held 6th
    Jan at his house. 7 Dec 1655. p 239
    A Court held at his house. 6 Jan 1655/6. p 244

Vaen, Ja: Certificate for land for his own transportation into this
    Country. 7 Aug 1654. p 151
Vall, Will. (This name may possibly be Ball or Tall). Headright of
    Capt Hen Fleet. 24 Oct 1653. p 89
Vaughan, James. To pay levy on 1 tytheable to Abra Weekes. 7th Dec
    1655. p 237
Vaughan, Tho. To pay levy on 1 tytheable to Mr Jas Bagnall. Also to
    be pd 455 lb tobo for his attendance on the burgesses from the
    levy by Mr Bagnall. 24 Oct 1653. p 94
Vause, Jno. Buys, with Wm Neale, 600 acres on S side Rappa from Rd
    Colman for 4000 lb tobo. 4 June 1655. p 206
Veale, Wm. To pay levy on 3 tytheables to Mr Jno Catlet. 6th Febry
    1654/5. p 174
    See entry Mr Tho Hawkins. 6 Aug 1655. p 209

Vincent, Hen: Wit Edwards to Dickeson. Exact date not shown, but
betw 16 June 1653 and 1655. p 148
Vivian. Appears in various and impossible spellings.
Vivian, Robt. His admr Clemt Thrush. His est in hands of Jno Gillett
to be appraised. 6 Oct 1652. p 16
Deceased. Late of Lancaster Co. Clement Thrush to admr his est
by order of the Governor. 10 Dec 1652. p 35
Inventory of his goods last in the hands of Jno Gillett , appr
by Andrew Gilson and Georg Taylor, include: 1 gould Ringe at
200. 2 sermon books 030. 1 bibel 050. Recorded 12 Jan 1652/3.
p 38
His admr, Clemt Thrush ordered to file inv. 6 Oct 1653. p 80
His admrs ordered to pay Ralph Warener a debt due of 300 lb tobo.
6 Oct 1653. p 80
His est to be pd 700 lb tobo by Jno Gellet. 9 Dec 1653. p 98
Inv of debts due his est 10 Feb 1653/4. p 117 :

Ralph Warener	0418 lb tobo
Clem't Thrush	0541
George Taylor by ac'ot	0180
Antho Jackman by bill	0670
Clem't Thrush by acc'tt	0300
	- - -
	2109

Waddings, Geo. Wit deed Bonner to Tigner. 6 June 1654. p 147
Waddinge, Geo. On his testimony Abra Moone has judgt agst est of Rd
Lake deed. 6 Oct 1654. p 164
Waldron, Hen. Headright of Capt Wm Brocas. 6 Oct 1652. p 16
Waldron, Hen. Wit trust transaction Chicheley for Wormeley. 18 Apl
1654. p 129
Wit assignmt Brocas to Chicheley. 28 Jan 1653/4. p 133
Walker, Jno. Wit Mascall to Rice Jones. Also Rice Jones to Powell
and Harris. 28 Feb 1652/3. p 54/5
Wit deed of gift Batersby to Newsan and Pine. 21 Mar 1652/3.
p 66
Walker, Tho. Attachmt agst his est to Mr Tho Griffin. 6 Feb 1654/5.
p 173
Judgt agst his est in hands of Capt More Fantleroy for 446 lb
tobo to Mr Tho Griffin. 6 June 1655. p 197
A non-resident of this County. Arrested by Wm Price for debt
of 600 lb tobo. Does not appear but sends a/c. Jno Sherlock his
security. 6 June 1655. p 200
Walton, Jno. Dif betw him and Wm Clappam' to next Court. 7 Dec 1655.
p 232. (Note: There will be a considerable amount of detail
concerning John Walton of Westmoreland County in Vol. 23 this
series - if I ever live to get it out, I presume I will. B.F.)
Ward, Jno. To pay levy on 5 tytheables to Mr Geo Taylor. 24 Octbr
1653. p 92
Ware, Mr. To pay levy on 5 tytheables to Jno Paine. 7 Dec 1655. p 239

Warener, Ralph. To be pd 300 lb tobo by admrs of Robt Vivian decd. 6 Oct 1653. p 80

To pay levy on 2 tytheables to Mr And: Gilson. 24 Oct 1653.p 94

He owes est of Robt Vivian decd 418 lb tobo. 10 Feb 1653/4. p 117

To have 150 lb tobo for a wolf's head. 6 Feb 1654/5. p 173

To pay levy on 3 tytheables to Mr And Gilson. 6 Feb 1654/5. p 174

To pay levy on 2 tytheables to Mr Felson. 7 Dec 1655. p 238

Warner, Eliz: Headright of Mr Tho Hawkins. 6 Aug 1655. p 208

Warner, Jno. Headright of Mr Toby Smith. 7 August 1654. p 151

Warner, Robt. Headright of Hugh Brent. 6 Feb 1654/5. p 171

Watkins, Richd. Buys, with Mr Tho Willis, 300 acres on S side Rappa from Richd Lewis. 4 Jan 1653/4. p 155

Watson, John. To pay levy on 3 tytheables to Mr Lucas. 7 Dec 1655. p 238

Webb, Gyles. Buys 681 acres on N side and 400 acres on S side Rappa from Toby Smith. 6 Feb 1653/4. p 128

Webster, Mr Rich: of Jamestowne. He assigned 2 bills, 1919 lb tobo, from Jas Williamson to Col Richd Lee. They are now paid. 4th Dec 1653. p 87

See entry Jon Woodward. 4 Dec 1653. p 87

Weeks, Abraham. Certificate for land for importing 3 persons into this colony: Himself, Jno Barnis, Tho: Chatton. 6th Oct 1653. p 77

To pay levy on 3 tytheables to Mr Rd Perrot. 24 Oct 1653.p 93

As atty for Tho Bemister is ordered to pay debt of 714 lb tobo to Maj Tho Curtis. Bemister having assigned a bond of 880 lb tobo from Mr Rd Husbands to Curtis which was not pd, although ordered to be pd 26 Nov 1652 at a Court held at Gloster. 6 Feb 1653/4. p 137

His land to be surveyed by Mr Toby Smith and Mr Abra Moone on petition of Da Wealch. 6 Feb 1653/4. p 138

Elected Constable. 6 June 1654. p 146

To pay levy on 3 tytheables to Mr Rd Perrott.. 6 Feb 1654/5. p 174

To receive levy on 58 tytheables from 19 persons, incl 3 for himself. 7 Dec 1655. p 237

Weir, Jno. Wit Powell, Paine, Snead transaction. 5 Dec 1652. p 48

Probates will of Robt Chambers decd. 6 Apl 1654. p 141.

Wit deed Paine to Killman. 6 Oct 1654. p 160

As exor of Robt Chambers decd ordered to pay Mr Geo Taylor bal of 300 lb tobo. 6 Oct 1654. p 162

Certificate for transportation of 10 persons into this colony. The list: Robt Chambers twice, Rich Wms, Ann Collins, Magda and Mary Steephens, Wm Hardinge, Daniel Elsmore, Jno Marke, Marga: Allen. 6 Oct 1654. p 162

Wit deed Gillet to Greene. 6 Oct 1654. p 167

To pay levy on 5 tytheables to Mr Geo Taylor. 6 Feb 1654/5. p 174.

Nonsuit to him in case vs Silv: Thatcher. Thatcher failing to prosecute. 6 June 1655. p 199

Weir, Jno. Wit Lawson to Lawson. 6 June 1655. p 205
    Wit Colman to Neale and Vauss. 5 June 1655. p 206
    Nonsuit to him in action brought by Sil Thatcher. 6 Aug 1655.
    p 208
    As exor of Robt Chambers impleaded Sil Thatcher for use of said
    Chambers' sloop from James River. Thatcher to pay 600 lb tobo.
    300 lb tobo to be pd by Mr Taylor, etc. 6 Aug 1655. p 209
Welbeloved, Matthew. Servant to Antho Doney. Jas Yates respited to
    next Court for refuseing summons to testify regarding his death.
    6 Aug 1653. p 63. (See Vol.1. Va. Colonial Abstracts.)
Welch, Danl. Certificate for land for importing 8 persons into this
    colony. 6 Aug 1653. p 62
    On his petition a Court order that Mr Toby Smith and Mr Abra
    Moone survey the land of Abra Weeks on 1st of March and report.
    6 Feb 1653/4. p 138
    To pay levy on 2 tytheables to Mr Rd Perrott. 6 Feb 1654/5.
    p 174
    In entry as Daniell Welch, planter, and Elizabeth Welch, sell
    Wm Coopland of Lancaster Co, carpenter, 537 acres patented by
    Welch 8 Aug 1652. This land on S side Rappa on N side Sunder-
    land Creek. 3 miles up the creek, E on land of Rich Lewis. Wit.
    Anth: Steephens. Cuth Potter. 6 June 1654. p 194
    To pay levy on 2 tytheables to Abra Weekes. 7 Dec 1655. p 237
Welch, Jno. Headright of Tho Griffin. 10 Jan 1652/3. p 24
    In this entry as Jno Wealch. Is given a heifer by Rowland Bur-
    nam. 6 Apl 1653. p 45
    Buys land, with Rd White, from Jno Pedro and Evan Davis. 23rd
    May 1652. p 45
    Buys land on Sunderland Creek from Edw Boswell betw 5 March
    1651/2 and 16 May 1653. p 118
    To pay levy on 5 tytheables to Mr Rd Perrott. 6 Feb 1654/5.
    p 174
    To pay levy on 2 tytheables to Abra Weeks. 7 Dec 1655. p 237
Werne, Christo: Admr of his est to Antho Jackman. 7 Dec 1655. p 232
Werington, Elizabeth. Headright of Capt More Fantleroy. 10 Janry
    1652/3. p 27
Wethall, Mr. See entry Tho Paine. 9 Dec 1653. p 100
Whettell, Tho: As attorney of Mr Wm Sheares gives receipt to James
    Williamson for full contents of letter of attorney in behalf of
    Wm Lea for use of Mrs Falldo. Wit. Tho Parker. 11 May 1651. p 6
White, An. Bequest from Edw Grime. Also his exor. 1 Aug 1653. p 124
White, Marke. Headright of Capt More Fantleroy. 10 Jan 1652/3. p 27
White, Richd. Buys land, with Jno Welch, from Jno Pedro and Evan
    Davis. 23 May 1652. p 45
    Buys land on Sunderland Creek from Edw Boswell betw 5th March
    1651/2 and 16 May 1653. p 118
    His land on S side Rappa bought from Capt Wm Brocas (See entry
    his name) is now seated. 28 Jan 1653/4. p 133
White, Wm. To be pd damages by Robt Mascall who had him and Edward
    Grimes "Causlesly" arrested. 8 Aug 1653. p 63

White, Wm. To be sued for a/c and debt of 600 lb tobo by Cuth Potter
     attorney of Danl Howes. 26 May 1653. p 87
     To pay levy on 2 tytheables to Mr Tho Brice. 24 Oct 1653. p 91
     Sued by Cuth Potter attorney of Capt Danl Howe for 958 lb tobo.
     8 Dec 1653. p 97
White, William. Son of Wm White. Given a cow by Jas Yates. See entry
     his name. 10 Dec 1653. p 103
White, Wm. His land on W side Corotomen adjs Wm Wraughton. 29th Nov
     1652. p 116
     He witnesses pre-nuptial agreemt Roots and Attawell. 14 Oct
     1653. p 121
     To pay levy on 4 tytheables to Wm Neesham. 7 Dec 1655. p 237
Whitehead, Eliza: Headright of Capt More Fantleroy. 1 July 1652.p 1
Whitlock, Tho. To pay levy on 5 tytheables to Mr Geo Taylor. 6 Febry
     1654/5. p 174
     To pay levy on 7 tytheables to Jno Paine. 7 Dec 1655. p 239
Whittle see Whettell.
Whitty, Capt John. Commander of the ship 'Richard and Benjamin of
     London'. See entry Syth Hayward, gunner aboard. Also that of
     Tho Crowded. 7 March 1653/4. p 142
     Judgt to his attorney, Mr Toby Smyth, agst est of Rd Lake for
     1016 lb of 'bisquite'. 6 June 1655. p 198. (Note: This was abt
     half a ton of what we Virginians disrespectfully call crackers.
     Perhaps hardtack and crack your old jaw sure enough. B.F.)
     In this entry as Capt Jno Whitty of London marinor. P of A to
     "my trusty and welbeloved friend" Tobyas Smith of Rappahannock,
     Gent., to settle a/cs. Wit. Rich Lake. Tho Borne. Rowland Lawson.
     19 May 1654. p 222
Wiatt, Edward. Wit deed Moone to Bourne. 26 May 1652. p 106
Wickocomikoe Indians. See entry Capt Hen Fleet. 6 June 1655. p 198
Wig, Eliz: Confesses immorality with Charles Snead. 6 Aug 1652. p 3
Wigen, Martra. Headright of Rd Perrott. 10 Jan 1652/3. p 26
Wilkinson, Tho. To be pd 150 lb tobo by Mr Toby Smith from the levy
     for a wolf's head. 24 Oct 1653. p 92
Wilkinson, Wm. Headright of Mr Row Lawson. 6 Feb 1654/5. p 172
Williams, Jno. Headright of Capt More Fantleroy. 10 Jan 1652/3.p 27
Williams, Marie. Headright of Jo Paine. 6 Aug 1655. p 209
Williams, Mary. Headright of Capt Hen Fleet. 24 Oct 1653. p 89
Williams, Nathan. Headright of Mr Ja Bagnall. 6 Aug 1655. p 208
Williams, Rich. Headright of Jno Weir. 6 Oct 1654. p 162
Williams, Tho. To pay levy on 2 tytheables to Mr Toby Smyth. 24th
     Oct 1653. p 92
     Ordered to pay Rawleigh Travers 115 lb tobo. 6 Feb 1654/5.p 172
     To pay levy on 2 tytheables to Mr Da: Fox. 6 Feb 1654/5. p 174
     He, with Alexr Porteus, buys 350 acres from Tho Best. 5th Feb
     1654/5. p 184
     To pay levy on 3 tytheables to Mr Da: Fox. 7 Dec 1655. p 238
Williamson, Edwd. Headright of Danl Welch. 6 Aug 1653. p 62
Williamson, Mr James. Justice. 1 July 1652. p 1
     Justice. 6 Aug 1652. p 2

Williamson, James of Redpoynt, Isle of Wight Co. See entry Wm Lea.
20 Sept 1649. p 5
See entry Tho Whettall. 11 May 1651. p 6
Justice. 10 Jan 1652/3. p 23
That Epa: Lawson decd owed him rights for 550 acres. The admr
ordered to return the names. 10 Jan 1652/3. p 27
Is pd 1540 lb tobo from levy. Does not state what for. 10 Jan
1652/3. p 29
Justice. 6 Oct 1653. p 77
Order that Court be held at his house on 24 Oct 1653. 6th Oct
1653. p 80
He bought goods in 1648. See entry Hen Montford. 12 Aug 1650.
p 83. Also p 84
He pays Jno Woodward 1919 lb tobo for Col Rd Lee for bills
assigned to Lee by Mr Rich: Webster of Jamestowne. 4 Dec 1653.
p 87
Justice. 24 Oct 1653. p 89
To pay levy on 8 tytheables to Mr Toby Smyth. 24 Oct 1653.p 92
Justice. 8 Dec 1653. p 96
Had difficulty with a maid servant of Mr Toby Smith. See entry
his name. p 98. 9 Dec 1653.
Wit deed Roots to Grimes. 8 Dec 1653. p 122
See entry Lambert Lambertson. 31 Jan 1653. p 136
Justice. 6 Apl 1654. p 140
To admr oath to Tho Meader who has been appointed Constable.
6 Apl 1654. p 141
Justice. 7 Aug 1654. p 151
Justice. 6 Oct 1654. p 162
Justice. 6 Feb 1654/5. p 171
To collect levy on 28 tytheables incl 7 of his own family. 6th
Feb 1654/5. p 174
His a/c incl in settlemt of Lawson estate. 20 Jan 1655/6. p 192
To pay levy on 4 tytheables to Mr Wm Underwood. 7 Dec 1655.
p 234
Willinge Creek. Adjs patent of Edw James abt 39 miles up on N side
Rappahannock River. 4 Jan 1653/4. p 184
Willis. Mr. To view Abra Moone's crop and report damage. 7 Aug 1654.
p 151
To pay levy on 2 tytheables to Mr Rd Perrott. 6 Feb 1654/5.
p 174
To view land sold by Moone to Dun. 6 June 1655. p 196
To appraise the estate of Jo Johnson and his brothers and
sisters. Robt Burton their guardian. 7 Dec 1655. p 231
To pay levy on 1 tytheable to Abra Weekes. 7 Dec 1655. p 237
Willis, Tho. Wit deed Harwood to Sharpe. 26 June 1651. p 119
Willis, Mr Tho. Buys, with Richd Watkins, 300 acres on S side Rappa
from Rich Lewis. 4 Jan 1653/4. p 155
Wit assignmt Keds to Pattison. 8 Oct 1655. p 219
Wit deed Keds to Pattison and Bridges. 16 Apl 1655. p 219
Willoughbey, Christopher. Wit bond 40000 lb tobo Epa Lawson to Rd
Bennett. 13 Apl 1651. p 9

Wills, Thos Mate of Capt Throwgood's ship in dif with Rev Jno Rosier.
   6 June 1655. p 196

Wilson, Hugh. Wit P of A Jno Jefrys of London to Col Rd Lee. 7 Feb
   1652/3. p 112

Wilson, Jafry. Headright of Rd Perrott. 10 Jan 1652/3. p 26

Wilson, James. Headright of Danl Welch. 6 Aug 1653. p 62

Winsmore, Mychaell. Ordered to pay Capt More Fantleroy "for a sloop
   lost". 9 Dec 1653. p 101

Witcheake, Joane. Headright of Sir H Chisley. 10 Jan 1652/3. p 27

Wood, Joane. Headright of Capt Hen Fleet. 24 Oct 1653. p 89

Woodcroft, Robt. Headright of Rd Perrott. 10 Jan 1652/3. p 26

Woodward, John. Receipt. 4 Dec 1653. For 1919 lb tobo from Mr Jas
    Williamson for use of Col Richd Lee. Due upon 2 bills assigned
    to Lee by Mr Rich: Webster of Jamestowne. Wit Benjamin Bealle.
    Tho Meader. Jenkin Hall. p 87

Woolha: Daniell. Headright of Capt Hen Fleet. 6 June 1655. p 198

Worksworth, Rich. Headright of Wm Brocas. 6 Oct 1652. p 16

Wormley, Col Ralph. His widow, Agatha, mother of Wm and Ralph Wormley, now married to Sir Henry Chicheley. See entry his name.
   18 Apl 1654. p 129

Wormley, Capt. His a/c incl in settlemt of Lawson estate. 20 Jan
   1655/6. p 192

Woulman, Jane. Headright of Jno Gillet. 6 Oct 1654. p 162

Wraughton see Raughton.

Wratton, Wm. Nonsuit to him vs Abra Moone who failed to appear. 10th
   Jan 1652/3. p 24

Wratton, Wm. Suit agst him for debt by Rice Jones dismissed. 10 Jan
   1652/3. p 24

Wraton, Wm. To be sued for debt by Cuth Potter atty of Danl Howes.
   26 May 1653. p 87

Wraughton, Wm. Is sued by Cuth Potter atty for Capt Daniell Howe
   for 303 lb tobo. 8 Dec 1653. p 97

Wraughton, Wm. Land grant to him and Rich: Flynt 200 acres on W side
   Corotomen, adj land of Henry Hacker, land of Wm White and land
   of Wm Clapham Jr. 29 Nov 1652. Rd Flint assigns his interest
   in the land to Wm Wraughton. 23 Nov 1653. p 116

Wraton, Wm. Has bequest from Edw Grime. 1 Aug 1653. p 124

Wraughton, Wm. Ordered to pay Cuth: Potter atty of Capt Da. Howe a
   debt of 303 lb tobo. 6 Feb 1653/4. p 137

Wraughton, Wm. Arrests Wm Catten for debt of 260 lb tobo. 6th June
   1654. p 146

Wraughton, Wm. Attachmt agst est of Wm Thomas 200 lb tobo and 2
   shillings Sterl. 6 Oct 1654. p 164

Wraton, Wm. Ordered to next Court to receive satisfaction for "buildings on the land apointed for a Court house and to be forewarn-
   ed from future buildings". 6 June 1655. p 201

Wroughton, Wm. To pay levy on 2 tytheables to Wm Neesham. 7 Dec 1655.
   p 237

Yarrett, Wm of Northumberland Co. Hired 2 servants to Mr Smart prior
    to 24 Oct 1653. p 92

Yates, James. Respited to next Court for refusing summons to testify
    regarding death of Math: Welbeloved, servant to Antho Doney. 6
    Aug 1653. p 63

    To be arrested for contempt and that Mary Doney who has remain-
    ed in Custody since the last Court on his accusation be acquitt-
    ed and released. 6 Oct 1653. p 79

    Confesses judgt to Mr Edw Conaway for 100 lb tobo assigned from
    Tho Roots. 9 Dec 1653. p 99

    He gives a cow "by the name of Dragletaile" to William son of
    Wm White. The cow "formerly recovered by the same Yates of Wm
    White for a debt of tobacco". Recorded 10 Dec 1653. p 103

Yeates, Jas. Arrests Mr Tho Brice for detaining his crop. 25th Oct
    1655. p 213

Yates, James. Suit betw him and Mr Brice to next Court for nonapp
    of witnesses. 7 Dec 1655. p 232

Yeates, Jno. Headright of Capt Hen Fleet. 6 June 1655. p 198

Yeomans, Edmd. Headright of Danl Welch. 6 Aug 1653. p 62

Younge, Robt. To pay levy on 2 tytheables to Mr And Gilson. 6 Feb
    1654/5. p 174

    To pay levy on 2 tytheables to Mr Smith. 7 Dec 1655. p 239

    To appraise estate of Paul Brewer. 6 June 1655. p 201

Pages included here 1 - 243.

THE LEVY
7 Decbr. 1655   *No Negroes had any tytheables.*

Although every person's name in the levy has already been shown in
the body of this volume the list is added in that it indicates the
grouping of neighbors. Later, when Lancaster was divided, many of
these groups disappear from the records.

County expenses are omitted.

p 234. Major John Carter to rec for 59 tytheables:

Major Jo: Carters plantations on both sides	21
Mr Tho Carter	4
Mr Marsh	4
S'r Henry Chichely Knt	29
Henry Rie	1

p 234. Mr Wm Underwood to rec for 28 tytheables

Jo Sherlock	2
Tho Meather	2
Tho Robinson	2
Mr Lambothson	5
Rich Tomlinson	1
Toby Hurst	2
Franc Goore	2
Mr Williamson	4
George Bryes	2
Mr Underwood	6

p 235. Capt Fleet to rec for 43 tytheables

Capt Fleet	16
Teage Floyne	1
Toby Horton	6
Ebby Bonnison	5
Mr Row Lawson	4
Willm Harper	2
Jo Brathat	1
Sam Sloper	1
Mr Clappam	4
Capt Fleets upper plantacon	3

p 235. Vincent Stanford to rec for 26 tytheables

Jo Taylor
Clappam Sen
Walter Herd
Jo Meredith   (continued)

LEVY. 7 Dec 1655. (continued)

Vincent Stanford's list (continued)
    Mr Kinsey
    Robt Gossage
    And Bower
    Jo Nichols
    Nich Houle

p 236. Mr Griffin to rec for 25 tytheables:
Mr Glascoocke	3
Mr Griffin	7
Capt Fantleroy	5
Roger Harrys	2
Mr Staines	5
Jo: Edgecomb	3

p 236. Mr Bagnall to rec for 27 tytheables:
Mr Bagnall	6
Jo: Bell	2
Cyprian Bishop	1
Mr Parretts upper plantacon	2
Jo Gregory	3
Mr Perry	2
Math: Humfrey	1
Mr Griffin	2
Mr Loe	3
Mr Jackman	3
Richd Jones	2

p 236. Willm Leech to rec for 52 tytheables.
Mr Curtis	6
Mr Connoway	4
the Lady Lunsford	14
Willm Leech	10
Mr Cox	3
Mr Tignoll	8
Jas Bonner	5
Willm Lucas	2

p 237. Abraham Weekes to rec for 58 tytheables:
Willm Tompson	2
Elliner Geyar	1
Willm Thatchwell	2
Frans Browne	3
Mr Cole	3

LEVY. 7 Dec. 1655.

Abraham Weekes' list (continued)
James Vaughan	1
Mr Parrett	6
Daniell Welsh	2
Abraham Weekes	3
Mr Burnham	12
Mr Patteson	2
Evan Davis	6
Richd Lewis	2
John Welsh	2
Sam⁺ Man	4
Robt Burton	1
Mr Hoberts	2
Mr Willis	1
Thos Kidd	3

p 237. Willm Neesham to rec for 54 tytheables:
Mr Davys	2
Capt Hackett	2
Tho Powell	2
Mr Dikeson	4
Mr Hawker	1
Tho Hopkins	3
Willm Abby	1
Mons'r Therryott	3
Willm White	4
Wm Wroughton	2
Mr Merryman	3
Charles King	1
Willm Neesham	7
Robt Thompson	2
Mr Beech	3
Mr Booth	7
Mr Brice	7

p 238. Mr Fox to rec for 52 tytheables:
Mr Stevens	4
Jo Robbinson	1
Mr Fox	14
Mr Sharpe	13
Mr Philipps	3
Mr Powell	6
Tho Cooper	1
Mr Travers	6
Ja Nichols	1
Tho Williams	3

LEVY. 7 Dec. 1655. (continued)

Mr Lucas to rec for 24 tytheables:
Jo Parmiter	1
Mr Lucas	4
John Watson	3
Mr Hawkins	5
Mr Rowsey	6
Mr Richd Lawson	5

p 238. Mr Felson to rec for 27 tytheables:
Robt Mosse	3
Ralph Warrener	2
Mr Tomlyn	4
Tho Rowsey	1
Mr Felson	4
Tho Cooper	2
Clemt Thrush	4
Mr Pettit	1
Mr Fellett	6

p 239. Mr John Paine to rec for 35 tytheables:
Mr Fleminge	4
Mr Taylor	6
Mr Ware	5
Frans Place	1
Jos Paine	1
Silvester Thatcher	3
Thos Whitlocke	7
Jo Eyres	2

p 239. Mr Smith to rec for 23 tytheables:
Robt Young	2
Willm Johnson	3
Jo Killman	3
Jo Bibby	1
Mr Smith	7
Willm Hall	3
Tho Payne	4

p 239. Mr Kempe to rec for 28 tytheables
Mr Bourne	6
John Bell	1
Jo Needles	3
Mr Kempe	5
Tho Hamper	3

(continued)

LEVY. 7 Dec. 1655 (continued).

Mr Kempe's list (continued).
    Rowland Hadway   2
    Mr Rigby   3
    Geo Kible   2
    Dennys Coniers   3

MEMORANDUM FOR GENEALOGISTS.

The suggestions here are very slight, but anything that can be taken as authoritative along these lines will be appreciated by great numbers of persons.

(1)   The parentage of Edwin Conway.

(2)   The parentage of Denis Coniers or Conyers.

(3)   The maiden name of Mary the wife of George Keeble or Kible. The relationship, if any, with Peter Rigby.

(4)   Note the Burr Harrison item in this volume.

(5)   Darby Hanrauley. Can this be the foundation in fact of the overtold Enroughty-Derby item? The spelling here would be all wrong anyway. Captain Fleet was not what you would call a fancy speller.

(6)   Fauntleroy - Griffin. Please note the deed of gift. It was not an accident,

(7)   Toby Smith - George Reade. Perhaps the most interesting item in this volume.

(8)   Mr Thomas Griffin. Mrs Thomas' vile remarks about Mrs Sarah Phillips may not have been in vain. It is possible that at this late date we should thank Mrs. Thomas.

B.F.